Pauper Voices, Public Opinion and Workhouse
Reform in Mid-Victorian England

Peter Jones • Steven King

Pauper Voices, Public Opinion and Workhouse Reform in Mid-Victorian England

Bearing Witness

palgrave
macmillan

Peter Jones
Nottingham Trent University
Nottingham, UK

Steven King
Nottingham Trent University
Nottingham, UK

ISBN 978-3-030-47838-4   ISBN 978-3-030-47839-1   (eBook)
https://doi.org/10.1007/978-3-030-47839-1

This Palgrave Macmillan imprint is published by the registered company Springer Nature Switzerland AG.
The registered company address is: Gewerbestrasse 11, 6330 Cham, Switzerland

PREFACE

This book has its roots in the remarkable MH12 series at The National Archives. This voluminous set of records encompasses all materials sent to the post-1834 Poor Law Commission, Poor Law Board and (from 1871) Local Government Board. In it, we find correspondence from poor law unions seeking advice or clarity on central rules and the practices and standards expected of them. MH12 also includes circulars, minutes of evidence gathered at the point of local inquiries by Boards of Guardians or central inspectors, the letters of advocates for poor people and, of course, copies of all the letters the central authorities sent in response to that correspondence. But the series also includes something else: the letters of social investigators and also those from paupers themselves. The AHRC project "In their own write", conducted jointly with Dr Paul Carter at The National Archives (Ref: AH/R002770/1; https://intheirownwrite. org), has been identifying and collecting the latter material. This massive undertaking (MH12 bound volume numbers in their thousands and have no index) suggests that there are likely to be between 20,000 and 30,000 pauper letters interleaved with other documents, though the real figure may be much higher than this. We are grateful to the rest of the team (Paul Carter, Carol Beardmore, Natalie Carter, Sue Hawkins and our three volunteer groups) for their work on the project, some of which makes its way into this book.

This rich material, allied with the ready availability of searchable online newspapers, has allowed us to focus on how the poor experienced and navigated the workhouse on the one hand, and how various constituencies of "the public" and "public opinion" came to understand and contest the remit and running of the deterrent workhouse on the other. In thinking about the volume, we moved away from current historiographical imperatives to view the workhouse through the lens of high-profile scandals, instead focusing on the everyday and ongoing disputes and problems highlighted by paupers and amateur social investigators. We emphasise continuities over time in some of the negative attitudes towards the deterrent workhouse, but also draw out the remarkable elision of the concerns and language of paupers and social investigators when confronted with the everyday realities of workhouse life. Both groups shared, and shared with a wider and increasingly vociferous press base, a sense that if the New Poor Law and its deterrent workhouse could not be overturned, then these institutions could and should work as they were supposed to. Crudely, we offer an anatomy of how a reform process developed from the deep roots of the early eighteenth century through to the urgent reformist agenda of the early twentieth century. And in this process we learn something very important indeed: that there existed a group of paupers who were informed by, and helped inform, press and public opinion on workhouses, demonstrating a remarkable seam of agency akin to the amateur social investigators who were also operating at the time. These people have escaped our attention. Finding them anew gives a very different sense of the New Poor Law and its totemic workhouses, one in which power was constrained and limited by the agency of the poor and their advocates.

Nottingham, UK   Peter Jones
                                                                      Steven King

CONTENTS

LIST OF TABLES

From Resistance to Reform: Changing Attitudes to the New Poor Law Workhouse in England and Wales

Abstract At the heart of Chap. 1 is a threefold argument. First, we note and trace a long history of public antipathy to workhouses in general and the principle of deterrence in particular, one stretching back to 1723. While public opinion (represented in pamphlets, failed legislation and newspapers) never coalesced around a singular workhouse reform movement, it is nonetheless clear that the opposition to workhouses that emerged after 1834 had long and important historical roots. Second, we trace a press campaign in periodicals against workhouse practice (though not necessarily against the existence of workhouses per se) that was much more widely distributed than normally allowed. Finally, we suggest that the conventional focus on resistance to workhouses in the first 10–15 years of the New Poor Law misses the gradual evolution of a much more coherent workhouse reform movement from the 1850s and 1860s. More than this, and perhaps surprisingly, there was also an associated rhetorical turn, with the sensational press descriptions of "workhouse abuse", "cruelty" and "inhumanity" characteristic of the 1830s and 1840s, largely replaced by the more measured but no less reproving term "workhouse scandal". This, we argue, reflects a widespread sense that the system had to be reformed from within.

© The Author(s) 2020
P. Jones, S. King, *Pauper Voices, Public Opinion and Workhouse Reform in Mid-Victorian England*,
https://doi.org/10.1007/978-3-030-47839-1_1

CONTINUITY AND CHANGE

In May 2014, *The Express*, a middle-market British daily newspaper, ran a brief feature based on a recently published book by Peter Higginbotham. The book was a popular, informative historical guide called *The Workhouse Encyclopedia*, and the title of the *Express* article was: "Before welfare: True stories of life in the workhouse". The actual tone and content of the article was, however, far more evident from the strapline, which read: "Britain's workhouses were so harsh they reduced their inmates to fighting over scraps of rotting meat".[1] There then followed, in the *Express* feature, a series of lurid, and very familiar, accounts of hardship and cruelty involving cholera, gruel, stone-breaking and bone-grinding, pillories and stocks, and drunken masters seducing young female inmates. Yet, interspersed with these well-known cultural tropes, almost hidden beneath the copious tales of misery and woe, were some less familiar snippets, such as the fact that beer was freely available in some institutions, Christmas dinner consisted of baked veal and plum pudding, and (apparently) "many workhouses made special provision for the inmates to pursue music as a hobby". Nowhere could the deep ambivalence that characterises both our modern understanding of Victorian workhouses, and the attitudes of contemporaries towards them, be clearer. The appetite for stories and "true" accounts of workhouse life has always been substantial, and it shows no sign of abating. Yet, it can (and, indeed, will) be argued that our expectations about precisely *how* these stories should read have tended to get in the way of an objective understanding of the lived experiences of the indoor poor in the nineteenth century. This book explores how this situation came about: it looks at how the workhouse came to be constructed in the public mind during, and even before, the nineteenth century; at the reasons why its reputation for cruelty and oppression has persisted for so long and has been so difficult to shift; and at the ways in which public debate about workhouses both informed, and was informed by, the experiences of workhouse paupers themselves. Our discussion covers the longue durée of workhouse history, from the enabling Acts of the early eighteenth century to the end of the Victorian period; but our main focus is the New Poor Law workhouse, possibly the most iconic institution of Victorian England and Wales, which emerged directly as a result of the reforms instituted by the 1834 Poor Law Amendment Act (PLAA).

At the heart of the New Poor Law were four changes that frame our book. First, the locus of welfare shifted from the parish to "unions" of parishes, and from largely amateur administrators to paid staff. More slowly and rather less smoothly than those behind the reforms intended, more than 15,000 parish administrations collapsed into some 620 union-centred structures. That is, the prospective and actually dependent poor would no longer know and inevitably have connections with the people who administered their welfare, something which the architects of 1834 hoped would generate a tightening of relief levels and attitudes towards eligibility. Secondly, the PLAA created a new central authority, the core function of which, once unions and their apparatus had been formed, was to bring much more uniformity to the administration of relief and local welfare practices than could ever have been the case under the Old Poor Law.[2] Centrally appointed inspectors and auditors ranged over this New Poor Law landscape. Although their numbers and powers were never really sufficient to achieve the tasks envisaged for them in the PLAA, they were successful (in the short-term at least) in achieving a third aim of that act: restricting the diversity and scale of benefits offered to those who were granted relief while continuing to live in their own homes, so-called out-door relief.[3] Finally, and most importantly for our volume, the 1834 act established a moral case that welfare for groups such as the able-bodied should only be given through enforced residence in the workhouse, with labour tasks attached to benefits and at a standard that would make accepting such welfare less attractive than seeking low paid work outside, the so-called workhouse and labour "tests". It is all too easy to overstate the speed with which new workhouse facilities were built, their capacity, the degree to which the able-bodied (as opposed to other vulnerable life-cycle groups such as the aged or sick) ended up in them, and the effectiveness and sustainability of less eligibility.[4] We return to these issues later in the chapter. Nonetheless, the workhouse has, as we have said, become the iconic signal of the New Poor Law. Indeed, it is arguably the most emblematic institution of England and Wales in a period that we might characterise as the century of institutions. Against this backdrop, it is striking that the early work of Anne Crowther, touching on the nature and experience of workhouse life, has not resulted in an avalanche of studies on the workhouse or indeed the New Poor Law more widely.[5] A small number of individual union studies, and David Green's totemic work on London, all of which stress the fragility of the 1834 reforms in different ways, have been more than balanced by a tendency for welfare historians to view the New Poor Law and its workhouses through the lens of scandal.[6] Telling the stories of scandal almost inevitably involves seeing the workhouse as a grim stain, with incarceration, punishment, control and abuse at the heart of pauper and community experiences of the institution.[7] Such perspectives meld seamlessly into early public commentary on New Poor Law workhouses (as we see below), but they are also founded on limited (often non-existent) engagement with the central archives of the poor law and particularly with the documents written by, on behalf of, or for the poor. These can offer welfare historians a first-hand (and alternative) sense of how ordinary people and their advocates experienced, understood and contested both the workhouse and the New Poor Law as a system. It is these themes that underpin the rest of this volume.

Here, in Chap. 1, we first look at the way attitudes to the workhouse developed in the long-term, arguing that the ambivalence and disquiet that characterised public discourse about the post-1834 institution cannot be understood without recognising that it had very long roots going back as far as the earliest incarnations of the deterrent workhouse. We then move on to consider the mechanisms by which this deep ambivalence blossomed in the mid-nineteenth century into an outpouring of public criticism in the popular press, and explore the relationship between that public dialogue and a growing "movement" for key reforms to workhouse administration and practice. Chapter 2 focuses on the work of one member of that "movement", Joseph Rowntree of Leeds, who (like his more famous namesake) dedicated a large part of his life to social investigation and reform on behalf of the poor. This Joseph Rowntree has, until now, been entirely neglected in the literature. Yet his labours as an amateur workhouse inspector and reporter on the treatment of the indoor poor were profoundly important in bringing to light many petty tyrannies and humanitarian abuses. Although he worked on his own initiative, Rowntree's modus operandi and particular preoccupations provide an essential bridge between external calls for workhouse reform and the campaigning efforts of the indoor poor on their own behalf. These are the subject of the final chapter, which takes the form of a number of case studies of paupers who engaged in extended correspondence with the central authorities between 1853 and 1885. Over many letters and many thousands of words, each of these pauper correspondents moved far beyond whatever personal complaints may have led them to write in the first place in order to bring to the attention of the authorities what they saw as systematic failings in local workhouse administration and the treatment of the indoor poor. In this, their approach was remarkably similar to social investigators like Joseph Rowntree, and the energy and fervour that they brought to their campaigns belie the traditional view of the workhouse poor as a cowed, downtrodden and powerless multitude. In order to fully understand the development and interconnection of these various trends for reform over the course of the New Poor Law, we must first look back to their conceptual beginnings in the century before it came into force.

WORKHOUSE CONTEXTS: THE LONG EIGHTEENTH CENTURY

The post-1834 workhouse was controversial from the very beginning, embodying as it did a clash between different conceptions of the duties and obligations of the rich towards the poor, and of the rights of the poor themselves.[8] But in many ways, the place of the New Poor Law workhouse in popular memory was sealed even before the first foundation stone was laid. It is too often forgotten that the template for the deterrent Victorian workhouse was established well before 1834. Thus, as long ago as 1961, John Marshall highlighted the activities of the "Nottinghamshire reformers" in the 1820s, and the opening of a workhouse at Southwell which was "constructed upon a principle of inspection, classification and seclusion".[9] The innovation was the brainchild of the Reverend John Becher, who came up with his plan "after fruitless efforts to regulate the poor", and the building was run according to a strictly controlled regime. Becher's workhouse consisted "of a centre, with a wing on each side. The governor, matron, and children, occupy the centre; the males are placed in one wing, and the females in another. A court [yard] is assigned to each sex".[10] In short, all the main precepts of the New Poor Law workhouse were already operational at Southwell years before the New Poor Law itself came into force: the classification of paupers into the "deserving" (the elderly and infirm, orphans, widows) and the "undeserving" (the able-bodied); the separation of the sexes and, therefore, the breaking up of families; and the close "inspection", or surveillance, of inmates' behaviour by paid staff. In addition, Becher's workhouse was surrounded by high walls to prevent paupers leaving and visitors entering without permission, paupers wore workhouse clothes and subsisted on a plain, but adequate, diet, and all inmates were required to perform useful work to the best of their ability.[11]

The strict regime at Southwell was not the only example in the final decades of the Old Poor Law. Winslow, also in Nottinghamshire, opened a workhouse in 1825 which was run on similar lines, as did Towcester (Northamptonshire) and Taunton (Somerset). In many ways, this timing is unsurprising. By the early nineteenth century, and particularly after the end of the French Wars, as the "crisis of the Old Poor Law" bit hard and deep, deterrent workhouses seemed an obvious solution to costs and assumed entitlements which were both constructed as out of control.[12] To quote Peter Mandler, following widespread public debate and a raft of restrictive legislation relating to parish relief, "[t]he 1834 diagnosis of the poor-law crisis was [already] available in 1817, and so was the prescription—the workhouse system—which followed logically from that diagnosis".[13] Yet, to really understand the evolution of the post-1834 workhouse regime, we need to step even further back, since the idea of the workhouse as a deterrent to those seeking relief had already been established under the Workhouse Test (Knatchbull's) Act of 1723.[14] This act allowed parishes to build, buy or rent workhouse facilities either singly or as part of a "union" and then either run them directly or "farm" the task to a contractor. Relief could be made conditional on residence in the workhouse and performance of labour tasks. How many workhouses were built, rebuilt or extended between 1723 and the next major Old Poor Law legal landmark of Gilbert's Act in 1782, is difficult to capture.[15] Estimates vary considerably from a few hundred to more than a thousand, and because parliamentary surveys in 1777, 1803, 1805 and 1815 were imprecise in their terminology and inconsistent in their line of questioning, no effective central record exists.[16] In practice, for much of the eighteenth century, defining what a workhouse was, locating its rules, and understanding where an individual institution sat on the spectrum between care and deterrence is a complex and convoluted task outside of the largest urban institutions such as those in Liverpool or St. Martins in the Fields.[17] Driven by a contradictory matrix of concerns and changing beliefs about the responsibility of the poor for their situation, local efforts to establish and maintain workhouses (deterrent or not) "came in waves", and often foundered or were short-lived.[18] Parishes might return several times to workhouse experiments and could enlarge and contract or repurpose existing accommodation as well as building or buying new premises.[19] The number of failed or shelved plans for workhouses to be found in local archives and press coverage by the late eighteenth and early nineteenth centuries is striking.[20] Nonetheless, by the 1820s, the conceptual and architectural landscape of the Old Poor Law was littered with "union workhouses" formed under private act or via the Gilbert Act, some long-established large urban workhouses and a swathe of institutions of varying prior or future longevity.[21] In short, the poor and those who administered welfare at the parochial level or through local incorporations and private acts carried with them a more than casual familiarity with the concept of deterrent institutions. The New Poor Law was, in this sense, by no means a blank canvas.

If the continuities between aspects of workhouse regimes under the Old and New Poor Law require more work, then the degree of ambivalence—and, sometimes, outright hostility—to workhouses on the part of some commentators before 1834 has also largely escaped attention. Whenever deterrent workhouse came into fashion, they were often (and increasingly over the course of the Old Poor Law[22]) met with a degree of disquiet and soul-searching among a strand of commentators and pamphlet writers. Less than ten years after the passing of the Workhouse Test Act, Londoners were already questioning the moral foundations for incarcerating paupers in punitive institutions. As Tim Hitchcock has argued, shifts in public opinion, in part stimulated by a well-publicised "scandal" surrounding the treatment of paupers at St. Giles-in-the-Fields, led those who oversaw London's workhouses to "focus their efforts increasingly on the provision of medical care for the infirm and elderly, at the expense of any attempt to impose a labour discipline".[23] The efforts of reformers such as Jonas Hanway and Thomas Gilbert much later in the century can also be seen as a response to the renewed interest in workhouse building, and they reflect a growing concern that "unfortunates" such as the very young, very old, and very sick, who found themselves in workhouses through no fault of their own, were being treated no better than the "undeserving" poor: the idle, the profligate and the immoral.[24]

By the end of the century, even some of those who were otherwise committed to workhouses in principle were questioning the way they were being administered, and their impact on the morals—and the morale—of the paupers who were lodged in them. According to Thomas Bernard in 1797, the workhouse test meant that some institutions were viewed as "objects of terror to the honest and industrious, and at the same time the favourite resort of the dissolute and abandoned"; and John Howard, the great prison reformer, noted reflectively that "I by no means approve of the idea of parishes giving no relief to persons out of their work-houses; for, even the best establishments of this kind have something in them repugnant to the feelings of an Englishman".[25] Of course, not all opponents of workhouses framed their sentiments in moral, philosophical or humanitarian terms; many local ratepayers lamented the per capita costs of indoor relief, while others rapidly found themselves at odds with the lack of parochial control occasioned by practices such as "farming" the workhouse to an independent contractor at a fixed price per pauper. Moreover, the fact that many workhouses were so short-lived and that parochial engagement with such institutions was usually episodic militated against any truly national opposition movement or unified alternative philosophy. Nonetheless, there *were* strong alternative views of the proper role and character of workhouses and, by the early years of the nineteenth century, as debates about the reform of the poor laws intensified, so the fractured nature of public positions on the principles and practice of the workhouse system became clearer. Thus, even as John Becher and the "Nottinghamshire reformers" were planning a new wave of deterrent workhouses, other voices were massing against them. The Whig MP Samuel Whitbread, on presenting his humanitarian (and ultimately unsuccessful) bill for the reform of the poor laws in 1807, was unequivocal: "I am an enemy to the workhouse system", he declared, "it has almost universally increased the burthen of the poor rate; and instead of adding to the comfort of the poor, or to the improvement of their morals, it has furnished seminaries of idleness and vice".[26] George Rose, who sat on the opposition benches, agreed. In a widely circulated pamphlet, he wrote that "[t]he avowed policy of workhouses, in many instances, is a mixture of maintenance, and punishment by imprisonment". He further suggested that "the abolition of workhouses" would be a "means of improving our system, which [should] excite our hope, and animate our zeal".[27]

In short, attitudes (positive and negative) towards the deterrent workhouse were already well entrenched by the time debates about the welfare of the poor intensified in the lead-up to the PLAA in 1834. Certainly it is clear that many of the objections that were raised against them after its passing were already common currency in the public sphere. "Workhouses are, in all situations, public nuisances", wrote the editors of the *Exeter Weekly Times* in 1827, "and, in agricultural districts, as unnecessary as they are impolitic":

> The benevolent intention of our ancestors, was, to supply the poor with Alms-houses, such as are in our back-lane; which are decent and proper receptacles for those, who, in the decline of life, are rendered incapable of maintaining themselves: but these humane intentions ... have been perverted, and parish prisons have been erected, in some situations, at an enormous expence, for the incarceration, without distinction, of the profligate pauper, and the indigent poor.[28]

This characterisation of the workhouse as a pauper "prison" was taken up in earnest by commentators in the press after the passing of the PLAA and it brings to mind the most notorious, and emblematic, image of the post-1834 workhouse: that of the poor law "Bastille".[29] Given the evidence presented here of ingrained disquiet about workhouses in some quarters under the Old Poor Law, it should come as no surprise that even this most famous of tropes about the Victorian workhouse was originally coined *before* 1834, during the agitation immediately following the passage of the 1832 Reform Act: "As to the working men", exclaimed a speaker at a meeting of the National Union of the Working Class (NUWC), "there were no laws for their protection, except so far as was necessary to protect them for the use of the property men … [and] when they were worn out, they were thrown to work in a *parish bastile*".[30] Very little of what was to come in terms of public criticism of the New Poor Law workhouse would therefore have surprised the audience at the Oxford Street Assembly Rooms in 1833.

Nonetheless, despite the various strands of opposition in the eighteenth and early nineteenth centuries, it is very difficult to pinpoint anything like a co-ordinated *movement* for the abandonment—or even the serious reform—of the deterrent workhouse under the Old Poor Law either in public or political discourse. As we have argued above, the voices ranged against workhouses were diffuse, informed by issues of cost and control as well as by deeper sentiments, and their target was, in a clear sense, fast moving. Transience was the leitmotif of the Old Poor Law workhouse which partly explains why the most critical voices tended to emerge in response to periods of intensified workhouse-building activity or usage, as Hitchcock noted for the decades following the Workhouse Test Act.[31] They expressed a general dissatisfaction towards the principle of incarcerating all but the least deserving poor against their will, but with one or two exceptions, these voices were more an indication of unease about the principle of general deterrence than a clear statement against indoor relief *per se*. As the editorial of the *Exeter Weekly Times* made clear, even among those who were most vehemently against the deterrent workhouse on humanitarian grounds, there was a degree of ambivalence about what to do with paupers who needed institutional care, and also how to deter the idle and importunate from claiming relief, particularly in urban areas and even more particularly in London. Hence, reformist voices such as Whitbread not only found themselves in the same camp on the "workhouse question" as people like George Rose, but also not too far away from Malthusian fundamentalists like the Reverend Charles Brereton. Although he came at the question from a very different angle, Brereton too believed that "[t]he arguments for the dissolution of [workhouses] are plain and intelligible. They appear by actual experience to have been expensive, immoral and unmanageable".[32] The result was that, on the eve of the New Poor Law, and with a century of dissatisfaction about the deterrent workhouse to draw on (including episodic riots against them), opponents still could not muster into anything like a coherent and con-certed opposition. Despite the many voices crying out that workhouses were expensive, inhumane, un-Christian and counter-productive, and that they demoralised even the most deserving inmates, the "crisis" of the Old Poor Law was such that even the most vehement workhouse opponents conceded that welfare was a problem requiring a radical solution.[33]

The exception to this rule—and it is not an insignificant one—is the broad coalition of political Radicals and Tory paternalists who opposed the New Poor Law in principle up to 1834 and who mounted extended campaigns against its imposition thereafter.[34] For a radical organisation such as the NUWC, the new regime, with the workhouse at its core, was viewed as a further assault on the rights and livelihoods of poor labourers following years of agitation for factory and labour reforms. But the imme-diate context for protest was the atmosphere of anger and disappointment at the limitations of the 1832 Reform Act (and the "great Whig betrayal" of the legislative programme that followed) as well as ongoing conflicts over weights and measures legislation, reforms to policing, and the impo-sition of the Anatomy Act.[35] For Tory paternalists, the threat was, if any-thing, even more fundamental: they argued that the PLAA was an assault on the British constitution—indeed, on the body of Britannia herself. In essence, theirs was a profound and instinctive opposition to the extension of the state into areas of local governance where they believed it had no place. These opponents resented the implicit usurpation of the authority of traditional elites by a national body—the Poor Law Commission—which would have the power to dismantle local welfare structures, impose central policy and veto the decisions of those who, they believed, under-stood the needs of their own poor far better than any outsiders. Richard Oastler, one of the most famous leaders of the agitation against the PLAA in the industrial north, was vehement, even vitriolic, in his condemnation of the centralisation of welfare. "[I]s it right", he asked an audience at Huddersfield in 1837:

that three stinking Commissioned funguses [the three Poor Law Commissioners] should be allowed to feed upon the root of the Royal English Oak, to drain its nourishment, and aspire to out-top its branches, and overpower it with their noisome pestilential effluvia? ... [Is it] befitting, that, now in England, the King's Commissioners should be permitted to skulk in the dark, from province to province, from town to town, pretending to establish a measure for Registration, when, in reality, their object is to bring "coarser food" or imprisonment [to the poor]?[36]

In turn, the language and sentiment of this broad rebuttal of the extension of the state found a willing ear at parish level amongst those whose power and judgement had been compromised and questioned, especially in the north of England where the logic of poor law reform was at best superficial.[37]

The strength of opposition to the PLAA meant that the first few years of the New Poor Law were beset by protest, obstruction and delay in implementing the reforms at local level. Nonetheless, the strength of localised opinion should not blind us to the fact that, not only were the Commissioners able to push the legislation through parliament with relatively little opposition, but for most of England and Wales they were also successful in persuading local officials to form unions of parishes and to establish Boards of Guardians relatively promptly after 1834.[38] In only a handful of cases was unionisation resisted successfully beyond 1840, and these examples were exclusively in the heartland of organised opposition to the New Poor Law, in Lancashire and the West Riding of Yorkshire.[39] For our purposes, however, it is far more important to establish how many Boards of Guardians delayed opening a New Poor Law workhouse after 1834, and how far this represented genuine resistance to it as a deterrent institution with roots, as we have argued, deep in the chronology and sentiment of the Old Poor Law. These are complex matters. Although it is possible to establish a firm date for the adoption of a New Poor Law workhouse in virtually all unions, the question of how far any delay, or apparent delay, was down to active resistance is often moot. For one thing, a large number of unions continued to use existing Old Poor Law workhouse buildings long after 1834 and although, in time, pressure was exerted by the Commissioners for guardians to establish a new institution on the preferred model, they "initially seem to have favoured the continued use of a number of existing parish workhouses in each union".[40] It was also the case that the Commissioners had no power under the new Act to disband existing incorporations of parishes legitimised by private act and/or by the Gilbert Act of 1782, and therefore to impose a new union workhouse on them.[41] There is no doubt, however, that in some unions a refusal to adopt a reformed workhouse was an active protest against the institution, usually within the context of opposition to the provisions of the New Poor Law overall. This is certainly the case in the north-west of England and the West Riding of Yorkshire. Todmorden, situated on the border between West Yorkshire and Lancashire, was the last English union to adopt a New Poor Law workhouse in 1877, having held out for forty years following unionisation. It was also, unsurprisingly, one of the most militantly anti-New Poor Law unions, and the guardians relented after so long a delay only in response to the Poor Law Board's threats of dissolution and the redistribution of their parishes to neighbouring unions.[42]

It is also the case that for some unions, particularly in Wales, foot-dragging, back-tracking and obfuscation were as successful in forestalling the adoption of workhouses as outright opposition.[43] In fact, the longest *delay* between unionisation and the opening of a workhouse was at Rhayader, in Radnorshire, which (like Todmorden) held out until 1877 despite the fact that the Board (which first convened in 1836) had originally bought land and sought financial backing for one as early as 1838. Rhayader's approach was an object lesson in the dark arts of prevarication, delaying a final decision again and again on technical grounds until it too was threatened with dissolution. At neighbouring Presteigne, the Board went one stage further: it was the only union in England and Wales to successfully resist building a workhouse at all, although this was a somewhat pyrrhic victory as Presteigne was finally broken up in 1877 and its parishes reassigned to Knighton and Kington unions.[44] How much of the antipathy of many Welsh unions to building a New Poor Law workhouse was based on moral or humanitarian grounds and how much was down to financial considerations or practical circumstances is the subject of much debate in the literature. Many commentators have concluded, along with Anne Crowther, that "[t]he guardians' own standard of living [being] low … they resented 'luxurious' workhouses" for the poor.[45] Others have suggested that a residual anti-Englishness—or, at least, resistance to the authority of an English body distantly situated in London—was at the heart of Welsh antipathy to the workhouse.[46] There is no doubt that the evidence does point towards these conclusions. But, as Evans and Jones suggested in 2014, there is also reason to believe that these considerations were adjacent to a deep humanitarian opposition to institutionalising the innocent poor in Wales, and that financial concerns and resistance to central (English) authority were as much weapons in the fight to resist workhouses as they were primary motivations.[47]

Whatever the reasons behind the delay in adopting or building New Poor Law workhouses in some unions in England and Wales, however, it is important to remember that they were still very much in the minority after 1834. Of the 563 unions for which we can date both unionisation and the opening of a reformed workhouse with a high degree of certainty, 380 did so within five years of the first meeting of the Boards of Guardians and a further 100 did so within ten years. Almost all of those that delayed for five years or more continued to use adapted or upgraded Old Poor Law workhouse stock which met the central authority's requirements (usually after further investment) in the interim before a new workhouse could be built.[48] Once again, without minimising the degree of popular opposition to workhouses and the PLAA more generally, it is clear those who spoke out against the deterrent institution *in principle* were in a minority even in the turbulent years during and immediately following the passing of the act. Yet, as we will see in the next section, the deep ambivalence towards the deterrent workhouse that was a characteristic of some attitudes towards it under the Old Poor Law did not diminish after 1834. In fact, it strengthened considerably as the central state extended its administrative reach through the New Poor Law. The rise of the information state went hand in glove with an increasingly critical "tribunal of the public".[49]

PUBLIC OPINION AND THE NEW POOR LAW WORKHOUSE

In a short reflective article published in 1992, Anne Crowther wrote that "massive investment, over 13 million pounds for [workhouse] building costs between 1834 and 1883, [created] an unstoppable momentum", and that, as a result, the workhouse "remained at the heart of Victorian administration". But she also noted that, although New Poor Law workhouses "proved indestructible", they were nonetheless "enormously disliked, even by the social classes who created them".[50] Crowther went on to explore the reasons for this deep antipathy. The deterrent workhouse was, she explained:

> supposed to invigorate family responsibility, but did so by breaking up families; it was supposed to encourage the industrious worker and discourage

idleness and depravity; but in the general mixed workhouse the sick and destitute were mixed together whatever their background.

As a result of these contradictions, "the workhouse system ... created discord even among supporters of the New Poor Law, and provoked a major clash of Victorian values".[51] Yet Crowther was also quick to point out that even its most determined critics were, to a large extent, hamstrung by the conditions that had created the New Poor Law in the first place. "The opponents of the law were vociferous, but had no alternative to offer", she wrote:

> To return to the Old Poor Law seemed impossible, nor did any doubt the need for some kind of institutional provision. Workhouses, once constructed, developed a logic of their own, since they represented a heavy investment, and soon began to fulfil the functions of hospitals and asylums.[52]

It is hard to think of a clearer explanation for the deep ambivalence towards workhouses in the public mind than this. In Crowther's analysis, once they were established as part of the welfare landscape, workhouses became both necessary receptacles of care and hated tools for the incarceration of the poor, and both of these positions could be—and very often were—held simultaneously in the minds of the Victorian reading and politicised public.

As we saw in the previous section, this was not a conundrum that was *created* by the PLAA. The "logic" of institutional welfare provision and its troubled relationship to deterrence was something that had exercised commentators and moralists for the best part of a century before the coming of the new regime, and the words of a correspondent to *The Gentleman's Magazine* from 1822 could easily have been written twenty years later: "Time, which has in some respects sanctioned the establishment of the Parochial Workhouse", he wrote, "has ... [rendered] any argument for its abolition almost abortive".[53] Nonetheless, it was a conundrum that was felt far more keenly after 1834. After all, no longer was the workhouse a voluntary form of deterrence or support: it was, in principle, compulsory, and theoretically, it was the key component of reformed welfare across the whole of England and Wales.[54] Despite the relatively straightforward passage of the PLAA through parliament, public debate surrounding the nature of the institution, and how the poor should be treated within it, redoubled in the 1830s and early 1840s. "Few, apart from the most irreconcilable radicals or paternalists, argued that workhouses should be pulled down", wrote Crowther; yet even fewer were happy with the role they were supposed to play under the new regime, and a long period of soul-searching was the inevitable consequence. This soul-searching found a perfect outlet in the rapidly expanding and increasingly influential popular press.

Historians have long noted the social and cultural significance of the rise of the "fourth estate" in the nineteenth century.[55] Following a reduction of the "taxes on knowledge" (advertisement, paper and stamp duties) in the 1830s, and their eventual repeal between 1855 and 1861, the number of cheap daily newspapers rose at first significantly and then dramatically in the second half of the century. Citing Aled Jones, Martin Hewitt notes that "while 1830–1855 had seen 415 new newspapers established, the six years from 1855–1861 saw a further 492, including as many as 130 in the 12 months after repeal [of Paper Duty in 1861] alone". The democratisation of print spread far and wide, so that by the end of 1861, there were "137 papers in 123 towns where previously there had been no newspaper at all".[56] But the impact of this expansion was much greater than the simple availability of news. With its roots in radical campaigns for a "cheap and unshackled press", it was always about broadening participation "in the formation of public opinion".[57] According to Joanne Shattock, contemporaries "emphasised the representative power of the [cheap] press: it reflected the views of a far broader cross section of society than Parliament, given the limits of the franchise", and this is certainly borne out by an editorial in the *Weekly Express and South Devon Advertiser* from 1857:

> We have a mighty work before us which will require every agent we can employ. Political and social reform must be secured; crime must be repressed; education must be fostered; the moral elevation of the masses must be continuously aimed at; the sweet voice of Religion and Philanthropy have yet to secure a full bearing; hypocrisy must be unmasked; and vice must be shown in its own image. For this good work the Cheap Press will be a powerful engine, and we have little fear that it will prove itself adequate for its fair share of the reformation of the world.[58]

Sentiments like these found a ready audience in those who were concerned about the effects of the PLAA. Disquiet and debate about the deterrent workhouse had been played out in the pamphlet literature and the limited organs of the press for a hundred years; but now, at precisely the time when the mobilisation of opinion was at its height, so too was the opportunity to open it out to the widest possible audience. Almost overnight, the "tribunal of the public", which in the eighteenth century had largely consisted of men of letters and the rational middle classes—"the collective conscience to which the state was accountable"[59]—was overtaken by an unstoppable and, to many, dangerously radical force: the opinions of the public as part of a larger movement that Martyn Lyons has labelled the democratisation of literacy.[60]

In this context, the best known, and most popular, critic of the New Poor Law workhouse is certainly Charles Dickens. *Oliver Twist* was published in the early years of the new regime and set the tone for the scrutiny of officials and the exposure of cruelty in Victorian workhouses.[61] It is a difficult—and perhaps ultimately fruitless—task to attempt to estimate the impact of a single cultural product like *Oliver Twist* on the public mind. But one measure of the book's success is that it gifted the newly democratising press a ready personification for self-important and cold-hearted officialdom. According to the *Oxford English Dictionary*, the noun "Bumbledom" (after the beadle who dominates the parish workhouse that is home to the young Oliver) first appeared in *The Express* newspaper in 1847, and this is borne out by a brief survey of the British Library's digitised newspaper collection.[62] However, it is apparent in the way the word was deployed in that article (an editorial on the Parliamentary progress of national sanitary laws which appeared simultaneously in the *London Daily News*[63]) that it already had common currency in public discourse.[64] Far more important, however, is the fact that its use increased exponentially after 1847, so that by the end of the century it had appeared around 4000 times in at least 542 titles in England and Wales alone (Table 1.1).[65] Although the term was only occasionally used in relation to workhouse administration and practice, the fact that Dickens' beadle gained such widespread currency over the years as a synonym for pompous and officious parochialism demonstrates both the appeal of his brand of satirical social comment, and the voracious appetite of the increasingly wide Victorian "public" for iconoclastic reportage and debate.[66]

In fact, the disparaging depiction of Bumble along with the workhouse master, the petty tyrant Slout, in *Oliver Twist* was not the first time Dickens had dealt with them in print. As Laura Foster has pointed out, they first appeared fully formed, albeit unnamed, in an early example of his newspaper commentary, a piece entitled "The Parish" that was published in *The Evening Chronicle* in 1835.[67] This realisation leads us to marvel still

Table 1.1 Frequency of selected search terms in English and Welsh Newspapers (decadal totals), 1834–1899

	"Bumbledom"	*a) "Work house abuse"*	*b) "Work house inhumanity"*	*c) "Work house cruelty"*	*Total a–c combined*	*"Workhouse scandal"*
1834–1839	0	0	0	2	*2*	0
1840–1849	18	27	5	22	*54*	0
1850–1859	81	7	12	9	*28*	2
1860–1869	616	23	108	38	*169*	68
1870–1879	754	7	4	4	*15*	111
1880–1889	1193	8	20	36(16)[a]	*44*	602
1890–1899	1305	1	3	6	*10*	983
Total	3967	73	152	117(97)[a]	*322*	1766

Source: British Library Newspapers Online (https://www.britishnewspaperarchive.co.uk/), accessed 14/10/2019)

[a]Twenty instances in 1886 relate to Louisa Twining's article, "Workhouse Cruelties"

further at the enduring legacy of *Oliver Twist* on attitudes towards the nineteenth-century workhouse; for although it has gone largely unremarked in the literature, Oliver's workhouse, with the powerful figure of the Beadle presiding over it, was explicitly a parish, rather than a union, institution. Given the timing of Dickens' article in *The Evening Chronicle* (28 February 1835, only six months after the passing of the PLAA), it must have been a depiction of a late-Old Poor Law workhouse, not a New one.[68] Here again we have a clear indication of a continuity of feeling towards the deterrent institution between the two regimes. As we noted above, there was little that was new in published commentary on the New Poor Law workhouse; but what did change was its sheer volume.

Despite the success of *Oliver Twist*, it was arguably through his crusading journalism that Dickens made the greatest contribution to the Victorian debate about the treatment of indoor paupers. In particular, he consistently took the workhouse system to task in his two magazines, *Household Words* (1850–1859) and *All the Year Round* (1859–1895). Both were highly successful weekly titles containing a mixture of short and serialized fiction (including *Hard Times*, *A Tale of Two Cities*, and *Great Expectations*) and social commentary; they were priced competitively, at 2d., to attract the widest possible audience, from the concerned middle classes to "working-class readers interested in 'trading up'".[69] The nature of Dickens' workhouse journalism is discussed at greater length in Chap. 3

below, but it is a measure of the success of his general approach that *Household Words* regularly sold around 38,000 copies a week (rising to 100,000 for Christmas specials), and *All the Year Round* sold 100,000 a week, and up to 300,000 copies at Christmas.[70] Yet these figures pale in comparison to other titles that carried the torch of workhouse criticism. For example, even before the mid-century repeal of taxes, *The Times* newspaper was selling around 50,000 copies daily.[71] This observation has real importance for the early historiographical depictions of the workhouse. In a lively exchange conducted more than fifty years ago, David Roberts and Ursula Henriques debated the question: "How Cruel was the Victorian Poor Law?"[72] Roberts took his evidence almost exclusively from the pages of *The Times* in the immediate aftermath of the PLAA. He concluded that the hostile reports were often exaggerated, sometimes false, and that, in any case, those instances of "cruelty" that could be substantiated were carried out *in spite of*, rather than in accordance with, the provisions of the PLAA and the guidance, let alone the sanction, of the Poor Law Commissioners.[73] In short, Roberts largely put any defects in New Poor Law workhouses down to the failings of workhouse officials and Boards of Guardians, suggesting that the Commission was, overall, a positive influence in mitigating the worst excesses of local tyranny.[74] Henriques, on the other hand, sought to bring the central authorities back into the frame, describing instances of "niggling parsimony" on the part of some Assistant Commissioners (who acted as workhouse inspectors), self-deception and disingenuousness on the part of the Commissioners themselves, and a blind adherence to the principles of the PLAA even when they proved counterproductive and unnecessarily austere.[75] She did not, however, dispute Roberts' observations about either the scale, or the nature, of *The Times'* criticism of the workhouse system in the early years of the New Poor Law. The fact that such an appetite existed for this kind of sensational reporting in the most successful and widely circulated daily newspaper in Britain raises important questions about the nature of commentary on workhouses in the press after 1834, and its relationship to the mobilisation of public opinion over the following years.

Thus, despite the deserved reputation of *The Times* as the most forthright and influential general periodical in its attacks on the New Poor Law, it was certainly not alone in its stinging criticism or in the occasional sensationalism of its reportage.[76] Even Crowther seriously underestimated the scale and scope of it when she suggested that the workhouse "was the bogey not only of Chartist pamphleteers, but of middle-class organs like

The Times, *Punch* and several of the Tory daily papers of London".[77] A brief survey of the many titles that proliferated from the 1830s onwards demonstrates that critical accounts of workhouses in the years after 1834 were far more widespread than has previously been allowed. For example, the subjective search term "workhouse cruelty" occurs twenty-four times in English and Welsh titles in the British Library online database (which does not include *The Times*) between 1834 and 1849, in a total of eighteen titles relating to malpractice at nine named workhouses. Of these eighteen titles, one is the radical *Northern Star*, seven were published in London, and the remaining ten were provincial newspapers published as far apart as Exeter and Newcastle-upon-Tyne.[78] In nine instances, "cruelty" at specific workhouses was reported, and these, too, were widely scattered: three in London (St. Pancras, Marylebone and St. Mary, Newington), five in the provinces (Gravesend, Wigan, Leicester, Coventry and Eton), and one in Ireland. In the remaining fifteen instances, the term was used in editorials about a range of subjects from the workhouse system itself to perceptions of Britain overseas, and it was used editorially in provincial titles as often as in those published in London.[79]

The sense that sustained criticism of specific workhouses, and the workhouse system overall, was far more than just a metropolitan or a radical concern is heightened still further when we include other sensational search terms that were regularly used by local and national titles, and broaden our inquiry to include the rest of the century. The phrases "workhouse abuse", "workhouse inhumanity" and "workhouse cruelty" combined, for example, occur 322 times in 164 local and national newspapers published in thirty-nine historic counties of England and Wales between the passing of the PLAA and the end of the century.[80] A significant number of these (twenty-eight) were based in London, but the vast majority—eighty-two per cent—were provincial titles. As with the term "workhouse cruelty", a number of "hits" in this expanded search appear in editorials and reportage on a range of subjects (mostly, of course, about the workhouse system or the shortcomings of the New Poor Law as a whole), but a clear majority, seventy-five per cent, relate to specific events at fifty-three different workhouses. Again, these workhouses were geographically widespread: nineteen were in what we would now describe as Greater London, but the remaining thirty-four were spread across sixteen historic counties of England, with a few scattered references to institutions in Glasgow, Ireland and the Isle of Man. Of course, the mere use of any of these emotive phrases does not, in itself, indicate that an editor or proprietor was strongly against the workhouse in principle. But, *pace* Crowther, in essence, this is the point: other than committed members of the Anti-Poor Law movement, commentators and reporters after 1834 rarely argued for the dismantling of the law or for the total abandonment of the workhouse system. Just as they had in the century *before* the PLAA, they focused their attention on specific instances of abuse within institutions, or on particular aspects of workhouse administration and practice that they viewed as iniquitous or inhumane. As we will see in Chap. 3, this approach has resonance with the way that paupers themselves conceptualised their agency in relation to the national and local state.

When we look at the frequency with which these terms were used over time, a clear pattern emerges. As Table 1.1 above demonstrates, they only began to be used in earnest from the 1840s onwards, which makes sense, given that the workhouse system under the New Poor Law took a number of years to reach maturity. Thereafter, there is something of a spike in frequency in the 1840s, which again is relatively easily accounted for by the sensation which was caused by the most famous workhouse "scandal" of all, at Andover in Hampshire, to which we will return shortly. Indeed, twenty-one of the fifty-four instances recorded for the 1840s relate to that one case. Andover notwithstanding, there was a steady accumulation in the usage of these terms in relation to the events at fifteen further workhouses by the end of the 1850s. But it is in the 1860s that the frequency increases dramatically: in fact, just over half of all instances of these highly charged terms in the British Library database between 1834 and 1899 occur in this one decade. As we noted above, 1861 is the point at which print taxes were finally abolished, so the rapid escalation in the use of these terms is certainly related to the huge increase in the amount of newsprint that was available beyond this point. But almost as intriguing as the sharp rise in their use is the steep decline thereafter, with only sixty-nine instances being recorded in the final three decades of the century. In order to make sense of this rapid fluctuation, we need to look beyond the sensationalism of our chosen search terms, and consider one final phrase which had even greater currency in the rapidly expanding press from the 1850s onwards: "workhouse scandal".

The use of the word "scandal" to describe maladministration in workhouses was all-but ubiquitous in the press in the final third of the nineteenth century (Table 1.1). It regularly occurred in reports of inquests into workhouse deaths or inquiries into accusations of mistreatment, malpractice or neglect. Indeed, it was often used to headline these reports and to announce them to readers, for example, in the cases of "The Liverpool Workhouse Scandals", "The Swainsthorpe Workhouse Scandal", and "The Bolton Workhouse Scandal".[81] The word "scandal" is, arguably, less sensational than "cruelty", "inhumanity" or "abuse"; but still, it is far from neutral. Rhetorically, however, they mean quite different things. The former terms imply purposiveness, and they tend to suggest a level of deliberate violence. "Scandal", however, has a much more diverse and wide-ranging usage. It can, of course, involve levels of violence (or "cruelty", or "abuse", for that matter); but it can also be used to describe neglect of duty, as well as moral crimes such as embezzlement, peculation, drunkenness and indecency. The frequency of its usage in the local and national press (absolutely, and relative to those other terms) and the fact that it became shorthand for poor practice or mistreatment, suggests that it was central to the development of a much wider, ongoing public discussion about the rights and wrongs of workhouse administration. This impression is considerably strengthened when we look at the timing and frequency of its use in our sample. Unlike those more sensational terms, which occur at intervals throughout the period and peak in the 1860s, the first instance of "workhouse scandal" in the British Library digital archive does not appear until 1857 (Table 1.1). Thereafter, its use increased exponentially until the end of the century, with almost ninety per cent occurring in the 1880s and 1890s.

When we consider the conventional narrative on workhouse "scandals" in the secondary literature, this distribution may come as something of a surprise. Most studies that have considered the subject have begun and ended with the Andover bone crushing scandal of 1845, to which we alluded earlier. The events are well documented in the secondary literature—one might even suggest that they have been picked clean—but the basic details are these: in response to rumours circulating at Andover, the Assistant Commissioner for the south of England, Henry Parker, was moved to investigate whether or not it was true that paupers who were set to crushing animal bones for fertilizer were reduced to gnawing on them for sustenance. In the course of his inquiry, he found to his surprise that such rumours did indeed have a solid foundation, and that it was "a practice with the inmates to pick out such bones and eat the marrow from them".[82] The case led to lurid headlines in the press and to further revelations about the cruel and inhumane behaviour of the workhouse master and matron. The fallout was swift and severe: the master and matron resigned shortly after the revelations emerged; Assistant Commissioner

Parker also resigned following criticism of his investigation; and according to some historians, an inquiry into the events at Andover by a Commons Select Committee led directly to the winding up of the first incarnation of the Poor Law Commission, which was replaced by the Poor Law Board in 1847.[83]

There is no doubting the lasting legacy of the bone-crushing "scandal" at Andover. It figures prominently in just about every extended discussion of the New Poor Law workhouse written in the last 120 years, from the Webbs' polemical account of Victorian poor law policy to Simon Fowler's recent popular history.[84] Indeed, for Peter Gurney, a central purpose of the New Poor Law was to ensure that consumption by the poor "was recalibrated downwards". Scandals such as Andover and that in Bridgewater union (which Gurney argues was centrally concerned with the "Gruel question") "helped instil fear in working class communities" and more generally the scandal-prone workhouse "continued to strike terror into working-class communities throughout the second half of the nineteenth century and well beyond".[85] Yet, as Samantha Shave has pointed out, in some key ways, Andover was merely the culmination (although a decisive one) of a much wider campaign against bone crushing that encompassed a number of English workhouses.[86] It was not an isolated case, and this was not how it was perceived at the time, even if the reporting of it was particularly lurid and the characters involved soon became notorious as a result of it. Thus, from a historiographical perspective, it can be argued that a focus on Andover has severely limited our understanding of the rich discourse about workhouse conditions that took place across the whole of the nineteenth century. Indeed, it might be suggested that the lens of scandal is more generally limiting for the study of the New Poor Law, even the New Poor Law workhouse. Recent work by Samantha Shave and Kim Price has very importantly moved beyond the newspaper record that dominates many accounts and begun to demonstrate the importance of public debate in relation to other notable "scandals" in creating pressure for policy change under the New Poor Law.[87] Yet, in common with the earlier historiography on Andover, their work focuses on isolated "moments" of crisis in the administration of specific workhouses: we still have a very limited understanding of the progress of what, by the 1860s, was an intense and rapidly developing public dialogue about workhouse conditions more generally, or of its influence on the formation and reform of public policy, and on workhouse practice.

Another unwarranted effect of the treatment of "scandals", such as that at Andover, has been a tendency in the secondary literature to focus on debates over workhouse conditions at the beginning of the New Poor Law and, at best, to downplay its importance in the formation of public opinion as the regime matured. For many, the events at Andover, alongside a focus on explicitly anti-New Poor Law reportage in titles such as *The Times* and the *Northern Star*, have become emblematic of the backlash against the PLAA in the years immediately after 1834. Yet, as we have seen, critical reporting of workhouse conditions and administration did not diminish as the century wore on. Indeed, judging by the usage and frequency of our search terms, it gained considerable strength from the 1860s onwards. But as the discussion above demonstrates, the *nature* of that reporting—and, by extension, the nature of the public dialogue surrounding workhouses and their administration—shifted over time. The fact is that not one of the many hundreds of titles in the British Library's online collection used the term "workhouse scandal" before 1857, not even in reporting the events at Andover; yet by the 1870s, its use was widespread in the local and national press, and by the 1890s, it was all-but ubiquitous.[88] This notwithstanding a sense that even prior to the Liberal Welfare Reforms and the development of benefits as of right, workhouse regimes were softening and many groups of vulnerable people were being removed from workhouse environments altogether.[89] Something clearly happened in the 1860s to change the terms of the public debate about workhouses and their administration. What that was, and what lay behind it, is the subject of the final section of this chapter.

THINKING OF REFORM

In much of the existing literature, if such a thing as a workhouse "reform movement" existed at all under the New Poor Law, then it came into being relatively rapidly in the 1860s and was largely concerned with the situation in London. The predominant narrative is that this "movement" consisted of middle-class philanthropists, public health reformers and poor law medical professionals who campaigned on a relatively narrow range of issues relating predominantly to children, the sick, housing and the elderly. Some of these individuals have themselves been the subject of study, and their work is referenced prominently in the general literature on the history of welfare.[90] Alongside commentary on the work of these pioneers of public health and institutional philanthropy, there is also recognition that the 1860s witnessed a series of well-publicised inquiries into the care of sick paupers in London's workhouses, and that they were prompted in large part by the campaigning medical journal, *The Lancet*.[91] As this account suggests, the overwhelming focus has been on calls for reform of the treatment of only the most deserving inmates, particularly in the metropolis. There is little suggestion that this may have been part a more geographically diverse movement, or that it was concerned with the condition of the workhouse poor more generally. In turn, focussing on a limited "movement" for reform fits well with the prevailing view of the post-1860s welfare landscape. This emphasises the withdrawal of any residual sympathy with the undeserving poor during what is commonly known as the "crusade against outrelief" between 1870 and the 1880s. The background to the crusade is well-known: demographic shifts and economic insecurity meant that by the mid-1860s spending on poor relief had risen significantly, especially in England, and this led to a period of retrenchment and cost-cutting.[92] The ideological foundations for the crusade were laid predominantly by "charity giving organisations [and] poor law reformers", and in particular, the London-based Society for Organising Charitable Relief and Repressing Mendicity (more commonly known as the Charity Organisation Society, or COS), who felt that the genuinely deserving had been badly served by a system that rewarded idleness and profligacy and encouraged dependence among the able-bodied.[93] This mixture of economic retrenchment and moral censure in welfare terms will be very familiar to anyone with a basic knowledge of the debates leading up to the PLAA. In fact, some welfare historians have suggested that the crusade was a powerful restatement of the principles that were meant to have underpinned the New Poor Law from the very beginning, but which had been lost in practice.[94]

One effect of the COS's work, alongside the wider crusade, was an intensified focus on the treatment of certain classes of the deserving poor. From an institutional perspective, a renewed emphasis on the "proper" (or effective) classification of paupers threw a harsh light on the treatment of those who were considered to be genuinely deserving inside the mixed workhouse, and in particular on children, the elderly and the sick poor. Unsurprisingly, many of those philanthropists and public health campaigners who sought to publicise the inadequacies of workhouse accommodation and medical provision for these groups were either actively involved in, or broadly supportive of, the work of the COS as well.[95] There was little conflict for some of these reformers in campaigning for the comforts of deserving inmates while at the same time supporting the ever-harsher treatment of the "idle and profligate": it was part and parcel of what has been identified in the literature as the "moralising mission" of the late-Victorian urban middle class.[96] In particular, they issued renewed calls for the physical separation of the deserving and undeserving in order to combat the eternal bogeyman of the mixed workhouse: moral contagion.[97]

A notable workhouse reformer from this period was Louisa Twining, to whom we referred briefly above. Twining was the founder and leader of the Workhouse Visiting Society (WVS), established in 1858 to encourage the formation of Christian women's visiting committees and thus the "promotion of the moral and spiritual improvement of Workhouse inmates".[98] The objectives of the WVS were threefold: "befriending the destitute and orphan children while in [workhouse] schools, and after they are placed in situations"; "the instruction and comfort of the sick and afflicted"; and, "assisting the officers of the [workhouse] in forming classes for instruction [and] the encouragement of useful occupation during the hours of leisure ... for the benefit of the ignorant and depraved".[99] Twining went on to promote (and, indeed, to establish) separate institutions for the moral and practical instruction of poor young women in London, and to concentrate on the improvement (and, in particular, the professionalisation) of care for the sick in workhouse infirmaries.[100] Yet, despite her considerable activity on behalf of these specific cohorts of the deserving poor, Twining—in common with Rogers, Nightingale and other workhouse reformers—never challenged the fundamental precepts of the crusade, or the COS's underlying philosophy.[101] The so-called undeserving poor—vagrants, casuals, and the able-bodied—were not within the purview of these key philanthropic individuals.

Yet, when we look again at the evidence from the local and national press, it becomes clear that the increased attention being paid to "workhouse scandals" throughout the final decades of the nineteenth century was reflective of a far more widespread, and diverse, concern about the treatment of the indoor poor than a concentration on the "moralising mission" of London-based philanthropists (and crusaders more generally) would suggest. Between its first appearance in 1857 and the end of the century, the term "workhouse scandal" was used in relation to 281 separate incidents in England and Wales. Crucially, only about a fifth of these (22 per cent) related to workhouses in the modern Greater London area. The remainder came from 146 unions spread across forty of the fifty-two historic counties of England and Wales. What is more, the range of issues that formed the subject of those scandals covered all classes of paupers and every aspect of workhouse life. The great majority of them related to the actions or neglect of paid workhouse officials, most commonly the master and matron but also (and routinely) medical officers, nurses, porters, schoolmasters and mistresses, and even chaplains. They encompassed instances of drunkenness, immorality, physical and sexual assault, corruption, dereliction of duty and, of course, cruelty and mistreatment towards specific paupers or entire pauper cohorts. The victims were as likely to be the able-bodied and the vagrant poor—the undeserving, in other words— as they were the sick, elderly or very young. In fact, these were precisely the concerns that preoccupied earlier critics of the New Poor Law workhouse system, and which were reported under the headlines of "workhouse abuse", "workhouse tyranny" and "workhouse inhumanity".[102] Such a preoccupation with the way that workhouse paupers of all classes were treated across the *entire* welfare landscape of England and Wales should lead us to question the relationship between what have hitherto been identified as the most important strands of workhouse "reform" and the great upsurge in public debate about workhouses in the press. How far were the pronouncements and actions of prominent middle-class philanthropists, framed beneath the shadow of the crusade and centred on the metropolis, actually representative of wider public opinion? And was their agenda for reform the only one of influence in the later-nineteenth century?

In order to answer this question, we must first address another: how are we to account both for the huge increase in the number of workhouse incidents reported in the press from the 1850s onwards, and for the shift in terminology away from sensational descriptions such as "workhouse abuse", "cruelty" and "inhumanity" to the more measured but no less reproving term "workhouse scandal"? Part of the answer to this question lies in changing knowledge about the scale and causation of poverty. As Peter Hennock and Alan Gillie point out, concepts of primary and secondary poverty and related notions of poverty lines filtered quickly into popular knowledge and discourse. While the methods used in early studies were unsystematic and observational rather than statistical, the sense that poverty was at least partly a function of the capitalist system rather than the fault of the individual or family gained traction.[103] At the same time, there was an increasing awareness that the landscape of social mobility that had underpinned the previous 100 years was under sustained pressure, through no fault of the efforts of the individual.[104] Variants of these views had always had some foothold in public perceptions of the poor, and as Lawrence Goldman argues, thinking on social reform can only be understood on its biggest chronological canvas. Yet, during the later nineteenth century, they began to have fundamental consequences.[105] Marjorie Levine-Clark shows persuasively that such narratives moved not only into the discourse of policymakers and social workers but also into common rhetoric, as working men came to contest ideas that receipt of poor relief undermined their masculinity.[106] In turn, while we have focussed on the coherence of a metropolitan "reform" movement (at least in its broadest sense), the changing nature of knowledge and the conceptual basis for understanding relief also sowed doubt and dissension amongst "poverty experts", social workers, social investigators and middling philanthropists.[107] Inevitably, these divisions were played out in the press as those with changed thinking became (or made themselves) a focal point for the discovery, analysis, and publicity over the "scandalous" treatment of the dependent poor. Chapter 2 of our study takes up this important theme.

In the meantime, a second answer to the dual question of how we account for the huge increase in the number of workhouse incidents reported in the press from the 1850s onwards, *and* for the shift in terminology towards "workhouse scandal", is less obvious but no less important: accountability. As David Englander famously noted, the PLAA was "the single most important piece of social legislation ever enacted", and "[i]ts radical redefinition of the principles of social policy fixed the parameters for all subsequent debate and discussion".[108] We (and many others) have noted that one of the most important aspects of that "radical redefinition" was the centralised administration of welfare in England and Wales. Despite a series of setbacks (including the fallout from the Andover scandal) the Poor Law Commissioners in London—Richard Oastler's "stinking Commissioned funguses"—gradually established a set of protocols and regulations according to which all workhouses were to be run. These were decided on a case-by-case basis, often in response to queries from Boards of Guardians which sought advice, in the early years, on precisely how to interpret the sparse framework established by the PLAA, and they were distributed to unions as a series of official directives and orders.[109] Beginning in 1847, they were also periodically collated and published for the information of guardians and other union officers.[110] As the duties of workhouse officials became more firmly circumscribed, semi-official handbooks were also published which set down the rules and protocols.[111] In other words, from at least the late-1840s onwards, it was not just the workhouse poor who were subject to the strict rules of the house: workhouse officials, from the master and matron down, were also now accountable for their behaviour according to guidelines and regulations set down by a national body of oversight. In the decades that followed, a recognition of this accountability—first, to local Boards of Guardians, and then, if necessary, to the Commissioners and Board members themselves—seeped into the public debate and this is an important reason for the shift in the rhetorical descriptions of maladministration and malpractice in the press. Individual instances of "tyranny" and "cruelty" came to be understood more clearly as part of a much wider set of "scandals", involving not only workhouse officers who broke the rules, but Boards of Guardians who failed to deal with such breaches and even, on occasion, sanctioned them. As the regime matured, the public ambivalence which had surrounded the deterrent workhouse for over a century focused ever more keenly on these breaches of trust and duties of care. The trickle of reports and extended debates over "scandals" became a flood, and touched all parts of the welfare landscape in England and Wales. On this reckoning, even the "reform movement" of the 1860s and 1870s, with its roots in retrenchment and the metropolitan "moralising mission", can only be viewed as a symptom of something much wider, but also much more diffuse: the power of public opinion and the popular press. How this power was exercised in some of its most important expressions—both by middling social investigators and the poor themselves as they contested their experience of the workhouse—is the subject of the remaining chapters of this book.

NOTES

1. *The Express*, 15 May 2015 (accessed online at https://www.express.co.uk/news/uk/475994/Before-welfare-True-stories-of-life-in-the-workhouse, 30/03/202; P. Higginbotham, *The Workhouse Encyclopedia* (Cheltenham, 2012).
2. From 1834 to 1847 the Central Authority was styled the Poor Law Commission (PLC), between 1848–August 1871 the Poor Law Board (PLB), and from 1871 to 1919 the Poor Law Department within the Local Government Board (LGB).

3. As well as seeking to reduce per capita cash allowances, Old Poor Law traditions of supporting payment of rents, provision of fuel and family allowances for children were firmly in the sights of inspectors and auditors.
4. See P. Jones and N. Carter, 'Writing for redress: redrawing the epistolary relationship under the New Poor Law', *Continuity and Change*, 34 (2019), 375–399.
5. M. A. Crowther, *The Workhouse System 1834–1929: the History of an English Social Institution* (London, 1981).
6. For summary of these micro-studies see S. A. King, 'Thinking and rethinking the New Poor Law', *Local Population Studies*, 99 (2017), 104–118; D. Green, *Pauper Capital: London and the Poor Law, 1790–1870* (Farnham, 2010).
7. On the lens of scandal see K. Price, *Medical Negligence in Victorian Britain: the Crisis of Care under the English Poor Law 1834–1900* (Basingstoke, 2015); E. Hurren, *Protesting about Pauperism: Poverty, Politics and Poor Relief in Late-Victorian England, 1870–1900* (Woodbridge, 2007); S. Shave, '"Immediate Death or a Life of Torture Are the Consequences of the System": The Bridgwater Union Scandal and Policy Change', in J. Reinarz and L. Schwarz (eds.), *Medicine and the Workhouse* (Rochester, 2013), 164–191; and P. Gurney, *Wanting and Having: Popular Politics and Liberal Consumerism in England 1830–1870* (Manchester, 2015).
8. The philosophical and ideological basis of the New Poor Law is well discussed in L. Hollen-Lees, *The Solidarities of Strangers: The English Poor Laws and the People 1700–1948* (Cambridge, 1998), 115–52, and K. Callanan Martin, *Hard and Unreal Advice: Mothers, Social Science and the Victorian Poverty Experts* (Basingstoke, 2008), passim.
9. J. D. Marshall, 'The Nottinghamshire Reformers and their Contribution to the New Poor Law', *Economic History Review*, 13 (1961), 382. For a more recent commentary see J. V. Beckett, 'Politics and the implementation of the New Poor Law: The Nottingham Workhouse controversy', *Midland History*, 41 (2016), 201–223.
10. J. T. Becher, *The Antipauper System; Exemplifying the Positive and Practical Good, Realised under the Frugal, Beneficent, and Lawful, Administration of the Poor laws* (2nd ed., London, 1834), 1.
11. Ibid., 17.
12. The phrase is, famously, Peter Dunkley's, *The Crisis of the Old Poor Law in England, 1795–1834: An Interpretive Essay* (New York, 1982), 4.
13. P. Mandler, 'The New Poor Law Redivivus', *Past and Present*, 117 (1987), 147. One key aspect of those restrictive prior policies was the attempt to increase the power and authority of the select vestry on the assumption that the biggest ratepayers would also be those most likely to

restrict allowances. See S. Shave, 'The impact of Sturges Bourne's poor law reforms in rural England', *Historical Journal*, 56 (2013), 399–429.

14. P. Slack, *The English Poor Law, 1531–1772* (Cambridge, 1990), 33–34; S. Fowler, *The Workhouse* (London, 2014), 28–29.

15. Gilbert's Act gave further incentive to the formation of "unions" but has often been interpreted as diluting policy commitment to deterrent workhouses in favour of creating institutions of care and containment. As Joanna Innes has noted, however, Thomas Gilbert was no humanitarian and his initial plans had been much more far reaching and punitive. J. Innes, 'The "mixed economy of welfare" in early modern England: assessments of the options from Hale to Malthus (c. 1683–1803)', in M. Daunton (ed.), *Charity, Self-Interest and Welfare in the English Past* (London, 1996), 139–180, and J. Innes, *Inferior Politics: Social Problems and Social Policies in Eighteenth-Century Britain* (Oxford, 2009), 99.

16. We are grateful to Joanna Innes for this point and clarity on the material that follows over the next few pages.

17. J. Bosworth, *The Necessity of an Antipauper System, shewn by an Example of the Oppression and Misery Produced by the Allowance System* (London, 1829), 31–32. In Liverpool workhouse (founded 1772), the poor were housed with "the greatest care and attention [being] paid to their classification", and "[a]ll the poor are employed according to their abilities". H. Smithers, *Liverpool: Its Commerce, Statistics and Institutions* (Liverpool, 1825), 295–297. On St. Martin's see J. Boulton, 'Double Deterrence: Settlement and Practice in London's West End, 1725–1824', in S.A. King and A. Winter (eds.), *Migration, Settlement and Belonging in Europe, 1500s–1930s* (Oxford, 2013), 54–80. For wider discussion of definitional problems see S. A. King, 'Poverty, medicine and the workhouse in the eighteenth and nineteenth centuries', in Reinarz and Schwarz, *Medicine and the Workhouse*, 228–251.

18. Mandler, 'The New Poor Law', 134.

19. J. S. Taylor, 'The unreformed workhouse, 1776–1834', in E. W. Martin (ed.), *Comparative Development in Social Welfare* (London, 1972), 61.

20. And also failed or shelved Parliamentary schemes for reform of the Old Poor Law, see J. Innes, 'The "mixed economy of welfare" in early modern England'.

21. Urban areas, and particularly London, dominate this picture in terms of our current knowledge, though "rural" counties such as Suffolk and Shropshire could also boast local incorporations and associated workhouses. See J. Boulton, 'Indoors or Outdoors? Welfare Priorities and Pauper Choices in the Metropolis under the Old Poor Law, 1718–1824', in C. Briggs, P. Kitson and S. Thompson (eds.), *Population, Welfare and Economic Change in Britain 1290–1834* (Woodbridge, 2014), 143–188;

L. MacKay, *Respectability and the London Poor, 1780–1870: The Value of Virtue* (London, 2013); A. Levene, *The Childhood of the Poor: Welfare in Eighteenth-Century London* (Basingstoke, 2012).

22. Joanna Innes points out that there were no large scale multi-county workhouse schemes floated between 1782 and 1834. See Innes, 'The "mixed economy of welfare" in early modern England'.

23. T. Hitchcock, 'The Body in the Workhouse: Death, Burial and Belonging in Eighteenth-Century St. Giles in the Fields', in M. J. Braddick and J. Innes (eds.), *Suffering and Happiness in England 1550–1850: Narratives and Representations. A Collection to Honour Paul Slack* (Oxford, 2017), 166. See also K. Siena, 'Contagion, Exclusion, and the Unique Medical World of the Eighteenth-Century Workhouse: London Infirmaries in their Widest Relief', in Reinarz and Schwarz, *Medicine and the Workhouse*, 20–21.

24. R. G. Cowherd, 'The Humanitarian Reform of the English Poor Laws from 1782 to 1815', *Proceedings of the American Philosophical Society*, 104 (1960), 329–332. For a deeper analysis see P. Fideler, *Social Welfare in Pre-Industrial England: The Old Poor Law Tradition* (Basingstoke, 2006).

25. T. Bernard, *An Account of a Cottage and Garden near Tadcaster* (London, 1797), 8; J. Howard, *An Account of the Principal Lazarettos in Europe* (London, 1791), 210 (fn.).

26. Speech of S. Whitbread reported in T. C. Hansard (ed.), *The Parliamentary Debates from the Year 1830 to the Present Time*, Vol. VIII: December 1806 to March 1807 (London, 1812), 910. For context to such reporting see O. Frankel, *States of Inquiry: Social Investigation and Print Culture in Nineteenth-Century Britain and the United States* (Baltimore, 2006), 46–50.

27. G. Rose, *Observations on the Poor laws and on the Management of the Poor in Great Britain* (London, 1805), 33, 36.

28. *Exeter Weekly Times*, 17 November 1827.

29. The notion of the workhouse as a "new Bastille" was most famously popularised by Thomas Carlyle in *Past and Present* (London, 1843) (see 4, 214, 311, for example). Such language found a ready audience because the 1832 Anatomy Act had allowed workhouses to sell the unclaimed bodies of the dead poor to anatomists, in effect placing the poor on a par with murders, whose bodies were routinely sent for dissection after execution. See E. Hurren, *Dying for Victorian Medicine: English Anatomy and its Trade in the Dead Poor, c.1834–1929* (Basingstoke, 2011).

30. *Poor Man's Guardian*, 30 November 1833 (our emphasis).

31. T. Hitchcock, 'The English Workhouse: A Study in Institutional Poor Relief in Selected Counties, 1696–1750' (Unpublished DPhil thesis, University of Oxford, 1985).

32. Revd. C. D. Brereton, *An Inquiry into the Workhouse System and the Law of Maintenance in Agricultural Districts* (Norwich, 1826), 19. See also P. Mandler, 'The Making of the New Poor Law Redivivus: Reply', *Past and Present*, 127 (1990), 199.

33. For a sense of the accumulation of this thinking see Martin, *Hard and Unreal Advice*.

34. On the "anti-Poor Law Movement" see especially N. Edsall, *The Anti-Poor Law Movement, 1834–44* (Manchester, 1971); J. Knott, *Popular Opposition to the 1834 Poor Law* (New York, 1986). For a more recent overview, and a useful local study of organised agitation in a key area of the industrial north of England, see F. Driver, *Power and Pauperism: The Workhouse System 1834–1884* (Cambridge, 1993), 112–130. See also A. Randall and E. Newman, 'Protest, Proletarians and Paternalists: Social Conflict in Rural Wiltshire, 1830–1850', *Rural History*, 6 (1995), 213–218.

35. Driver, *Power and Pauperism*, 113–114; E. Royle, *Revolutionary Britannia? Reflections on the Threat of Revolution in Britain, 1789–1848* (Manchester, 2000), 97.

36. *Damnation! Eternal Damnation to the Fiend-Begotten, "Coarser Food" New Poor Law. A Speech by Richard Oastler* (London, 1837), 7.

37. See S. A. King, 'Rights, duties and practice in the transition between the Old and New Poor Laws 1820–1860s', in P. Jones and S. A. King (eds.), *Obligation, Entitlement and Dispute under the English Poor Laws, 1600–1900* (Newcastle, 2015), 263–291.

38. M. A. Crowther, 'The Workhouse', *Proceedings of the British Academy*, 78 (1992), 183–184.

39. The locations that delayed unionisation until after 1840 (with the eventual date of unionisation in brackets) are: Liverpool (1841), Leeds (1844), Ashbourne in Derbyshire (1845), Barnsley (1850), Hemsworth (1850), Ripon (1852), and Pontefract (1862). The discussion about dates of unionisation, and that which follows relating to delays in adopting New Poor Law workhouses, are based on an extensive database compiled predominantly from data gathered by Peter Higginbotham for his website http://www.workhouses.org.uk. For a fuller explanation of the workhouse database, see M. Evans and P. Jones, '"A Stubborn and Intractable Body": Resistance to the Workhouse in Wales, 1834–1877', *Family and Community History*, 17 (2014), Appendix 1.

40. Driver, *Power and Pauperism*, 59. Continued usage often involved further investment in enlargement or internal modifications to accommodate the basic principles of 1834.
41. For an excellent description of the gaining and working of local acts see J. Shaw (ed.), *The Loes and Wilford Poor Law Incorporation, 1765–1826* (Woodbridge, 2019).
42. Edsall, *Anti-Poor Law Movement*, 224; N. Longmate, *The Workhouse: A Social History* (London, 1974), 81.
43. For the best description of this process, see G. Hooker, 'Llandilofawr poor law union 1836–1886: "The most difficult union in Wales"' (Unpublished PhD thesis, University of Leicester, 2013).
44. Evans and Jones, '"A Stubborn and Intractable Body"', 105.
45. Crowther, *Workhouse System*, 47.
46. A. Brundage, *The Making of the New Poor Law: The Politics of Inquiry, Enactment and Implementation 1832–39* (New Brunswick, NJ, 1978), 47; Edsall, *Anti-Poor Law Movement*, 129; A. Kidd, *State, Society and the Poor in Nineteenth-Century England* (Basingstoke, 1999), 30.
47. Evans and Jones, '"A Stubborn and Intractable Body"', 110. For a more ambivalent view of the ideological foundation of Welsh resistance to the New Poor Law, especially in the later-nineteenth century, see A. Croll, '"Reconciled Gradually to the System of Indoor Relief": The Poor law in Wales during the 'Crusade Against Out-Relief', c.1870–1890', *Family and Community History*, 20 (2017), 121–144.
48. Workhouse Database. Only 26 of the 563 unions delayed the use of a workhouse of any kind beyond five years, and ten of those were in Wales.
49. On the information state see P. Harling, *The Modern British State* (Cambridge, 2001) and E Higgs, *The Information State in England: The Central Collection of Information on Citizens since 1500* (Basingstoke, 2003). For a comprehensive discussion of the tribunal of the public see C. Brant, '"The tribunal of the public": Eighteenth century letters and the politics of vindication', in C. Bland and M. Cross (eds.), *Gender and Politics in the Age of Letter Writing, 1750–2000* (Aldershot, 2004), 15–28.
50. Crowther, 'The Workhouse', 184.
51. Ibid.
52. Ibid., 189–190.
53. 'A. H.', 'On Workhouses and Lots of Land', *The Gentleman's Magazine*, Vol. 92 (July 1822), 28.
54. In practice, and as all modern commentators on the New Poor Law have acknowledged, in most places, at most times and for most life-cycle groups outdoor relief remained the cornerstone of welfare. For the importance of the crusade against outdoor relief as an attempt to change the balance back to indoor relief see Hurren, *Protesting*.

55. For a summary, see J. Grande, *William Cobbett, the Press and Rural England: Radicalism and the Fourth Estate, 1792–1835* (Basingstoke, 2014).

56. M. Hewitt, *The Dawn of the Cheap Press in Victorian Britain: The End of the "Taxes on Knowledge", 1849–1869* (London, 2013), 98.

57. Memorandum from the Association of Working Men to Procure a Cheap and Honest Press, April 1836, quoted in J. Black, *The English Press, 1621–1861* (Stroud, 2001), 177–178.

58. Introduction to J. Shattock (ed.), *Journalism and the Periodical Press* (Cambridge, 2019), 2; *Weekly Express and South Devon Advertiser*, 8 January 1857, quoted in Black, *The English Press*, 185.

59. A. J. La Vopa, 'Conceiving a Public: Ideas and Society in Eighteenth-Century Europe', *Journal of Modern History*, 64 (1992), 83. Defining "the public" envisaged by terms such as "tribunal of the public" or "public opinion" is by no means easy. W. Selinger and G. Conti, 'Reappraising Walter Bagehot's Liberalism: Discussion, Public Opinion, and the Meaning of Parliamentary Government', *History of European Ideas*, 41 (2015), 264–291 provide an exemplary discussion of such complexity. In this book we follow Selinger and Conti and understand public opinion in its broadest sweep, as a widely held and traceable (though not necessarily coherent or chronologically, rhetorically and conceptually uniform) sentiment on an issue or set of related issues that can be seen to have an audience outside the group that immediately holds such sentiments.

60. M. Lyons, *The Writing Culture of Ordinary People in Europe c.1860–1920* (Cambridge, 2013).

61. *Oliver Twist, or the Parish Boy's Progress* was originally published in twenty-four monthly instalments in Bentley's Miscellany between February 1837 and April 1839.

62. *Oxford English Dictionary* online: https://www.oed.com (accessed 19/10/2019); The British Newspaper Archive, https://www.british-newspaperarchive.co.uk/ (accessed 19/10/2019).

63. *The Express* and *London Daily News*, 12 May 1847.

64. The new measures, noted the writer, "will rout the bugbears of Bumbledom".

65. https://www.britishnewspaperarchive.co.uk/ (accessed 14/10/2019). The word "Bumbledom" also appeared in Scottish and Irish titles (439 times in the former, and 293 in the latter). The following discussions based on searches and search terms in the British Library online newspaper collection are not intended to be exhaustive or definitive. Issues such as the exponential increase in the number of newspaper titles over the nineteenth century, and the limits to the coverage of the British Library's current digital collection, mean that any conclusions based on the use of

its search engine can only be indicative. We believe, however, that they are nonetheless highly persuasive, especially when considered alongside the other evidence presented here.

66. For a good example of the term's longevity, see R. Porter, *London: A Social History* (London: 1995), Chapter 10: 'Bumbledom? London's Politics, 1800–1890'.

67. L. Foster, 'The Representation of the Workhouse in Nineteenth-Century Culture' (Unpublished PhD thesis, University of Cardiff, 2014), 112–113.

68. The Poor Law Amendment Act received royal assent on 14 August 1834.

69. L. Brake & M. Demoor (eds.), *Dictionary of Nineteenth-Century Journalism in Great Britain and Ireland* (Ghent, 2009), 11, 292–293. See also, L. Foster, "Probing the workhouse in All the Year Round', in H. Mackenzie and B. Winyard (eds.), *Charles Dickens and the Mid-Victorian Press, 1850–1870* (Kindle eBook: Buckingham, 2013), loc.1828–2014.

70. Brake and Demoor, *Dictionary*, 11, 292.

71. Black, *English Press*, 142.

72. R. Roberts, 'How Cruel was the Victorian Poor Law', *Historical Journal*, 6 (1963), 97–107; U. Henriques, 'How Cruel was the Victorian Poor Law', *Historical Journal*, 11 (1968), 365–371.

73. Roberts, 'How Cruel', 97–100, 103–105.

74. Ibid., 103–105.

75. Henriques, 'How Cruel', 363–365, 369.

76. See, for example, Edsall, *Anti-Poor Law Movement*, 17, 120; Green, *Pauper Capital*, 107; E. Hadley, *Melodramatic Tactics: Theatricalized Dissent in the English Marketplace, 1800–1885* (Stanford, 1995), 7–78.

77. Crowther, 'The Workhouse', 192.

78. https://www.britishnewspaperarchive.co.uk/ (accessed 14/10/2019). The London titles are: *London Evening Standard, The Sun, Morning Advertiser, Morning Post, Evening Mail, The Globe* and *The Tablet*. The full list of provincial titles is: *West Kent Guardian, Liverpool Mail, Leicestershire Mercury, Exeter and Plymouth Gazette, Suffolk Chronicle, Coventry Herald, Newcastle Guardian and Tyne Mercury, Worcestershire Chronicle* and *Preston Chronicle*.

79. For comparison, the phrase "workhouse cruelty" only appeared in *The Times* twice in the whole period under consideration: once in 1837 and again in 1844. The British Library database reveals only one instance of the phrase "workhouse cruelty" pre-1834 and even that was in 1832. Other pre-1834 instances of the phrase can be traced via tools such as Google Books (in for instance *Annals of Agriculture* in 1799, and we are grateful to Joanna Innes for this reference), but the numbers are still small.

80. This figure has been adjusted downwards to remove twenty instances of the term "workhouse cruelty" which relate solely to an article of that title by Louisa Twining (a well-known workhouse reformer about whom we will have much more to say shortly), which appeared in 1886 and was widely reviewed elsewhere in the press. See L. Twining, 'Workhouse Cruelties', *Nineteenth Century*, 20 (1886), 709–714.

81. *Liverpool Echo*, 24 August 1880; *Norfolk Chronicle*, 23 August 1873; *Lancaster Gazette*, 4 January 1890

82. Assistant Commissioner Henry Parker, quoted in S. A. Shave, *Pauper Policies: Poor Law Practice in England, 1780–1850* (Manchester, 2017), 225.

83. Longmate, *The Workhouse*, 133–134; R. Wells, review of P. Carter (ed.), *Bradford Poor Law Union: Papers and Correspondence with the Poor Law Commission* (Woodbridge, 2004), in *English Historical Review*, 121 (2006), 233; D. Roberts, review of I. Anstruther, *The Scandal of the Andover Workhouse: A Documentary Study of Events, 1834–1847* (London, 1973), in *Victorian Studies*, 17 (1973), 237.

84. S. and B. Webb, *English Poor Law Policy* (London, 1913) 75, 132; Fowler, *The Workhouse*, viii-x, 54–58. See also I. Anstruther, *The Scandal of the Andover Workhouse*; Longmate, *The Workhouse*, 122–133; and even Crowther, *Workhouse System*, 30, 198.

85. Gurney, *Wanting and Having*, 66, 77, 94–95.

86. Shave, *Pauper Policies*, 221–231.

87. Shave, '"Immediate Death"', 164–191; Shave, *Pauper Policies*, 197–247; and S. Shave, '"Great Inhumanity"': Scandal, Child Punishment and Policymaking in the Early Years of the New Poor Law Workhouse System', *Continuity and Change*, 33 (2018), 339–363. K. Price, '"Where is the Fault?"': The Starvation of Edward Cooper at the Isle of Wight Workhouse in 1877', *Social history of Medicine*, 26 (2012), 21–37; and Price, *Medical Negligence*, 49–72.

88. As of October 2019, the British Newspaper Online Archive holds digital material for 1107 titles, dating from 1708 to the year 2000. The fact that the specific term "workhouse scandal" does not appear in any of them before 1857 suggests that its use in relation to the events at Andover is a product of the historiography, not of contemporary reportage. The word "scandal" did appear once or twice in that reportage, but exclusively in relation to the "scandalous behaviour" of the workhouse master.

89. See S. A. King, *Women, Welfare and Local Politics 1880–1920: "We Might be Trusted"* (Brighton, 2005).

90. See, for example, T. Deane, 'Late Nineteenth-Century Philanthropy: the Case of Louisa Twining', in A. Digby and J. Stewart (eds.), *Gender, Health and Welfare* (London, 1996), 122–142; T. Deane, 'The

Professionalisation of Philanthropy: the case of Louisa Twining, 1820–1912' (Unpublished PhD thesis, University of Sussex, 2005); L. McDonald, *Florence Nightingale at First Hand: Vision, Power and Legacy* (London, 2010), esp. chapter five; L. Penner, *Victorian Medicine and Social Reform: Florence Nightingale among the Novelists* (New York, 2010), esp. chapter two; Price, *Medical Negligence*, esp. chapters four and six; R. Richardson and B. Hurwitz, 'Joseph Rogers and the Reform of Workhouse Medicine', *British Medical Journal*, 299 (1989), 1507–1510.

91. Crowther, *The Workhouse System*, 160–161; Driver, *Power and Pauperism*, 69; Longmate, *The Workhouse*, 204–206; Price, *Medical Negligence*, 58–63. See also the many references to Twining, Rogers and Nightingale in Crowther, *Workhouse System*; Driver, *Power and Pauperism*; and Longmate, *The Workhouse*.

92. See especially, Hurren, *Protesting*, chapter two; M. McKinnon, 'English Poor Law Policy and the Crusade Against Outrelief', *The Journal of Economic History*, 47 (1987), 603–625; K. Williams, *From Pauperism to Poverty* (Oxford, 1981), chapter three. For the situation in Wales, see Croll, '"Reconciled Gradually to the System of Indoor Relief"'.

93. Hurren, *Protesting*, 59.

94. King, *Women, Welfare*, 37–41. Others have argued that the economic and ideological underpinnings of the crusade were very much a product of the post-1860s welfare landscape. See, for example, Hurren, *Protesting*; McKinnon, 'English Poor Law Policy'.

95. See L. McDonald, *Florence Nightingale: An Introduction to her Life and Family*, Vol. 1 (Waterloo, ON, 2001), 70–71; Price, *Medical Negligence*, 108–111.

96. G. Ginn, *Culture, Philanthropy and the Poor in Late-Victorian Britain* (London, 2017), 3–5.

97. Crowther, *Workhouse System*, 84; Driver, *Power and Pauperism*, 65.

98. *Journal of the Workhouse Visiting Society* (London, 1859), No.2, 3. In keeping with the general thrust of workhouse "reform" during this period, Twining was a co-founder of the Workhouse Nursing Association in 1874, an organisation in which Florence Nightingale also maintained a keen interest. See Deane, 'Late Nineteenth-Century Philanthropy', 135.

99. *Journal of the Workhouse Visiting Society*, No. 2, 3.

100. Deane, 'Late Nineteenth-Century Philanthropy'.

101. Indeed, Twining is known to have been a strong supporter of the COS. Deane, 'Professionalisation of Philanthropy', 148–149.

102. R. Breton, 'Portraits of the poor in early nineteenth century radical journalism', *Journal of Victorian Culture*, 21 (2016), 168–183.

103. E. P. Hennock, 'The measurement of urban poverty: From the metropolis to the nation, 1880–1920', *Economic History Review*, 40 (1987),

208–227; A. Gillie, 'The origin of the poverty line', *Economic History Review*, 49 (1996), 715–730.

104. N. Boberg Fazlić and P. Sharp, 'North and south: Long run social mobility in England and attitudes towards welfare', *Cliometrica*, 12 (2018), 251–276.

105. L. Goldman, 'Social reform and the pressures of "progress" on Parliament, 1660–1914', *Parliamentary History*, (2018), 72–88.

106. M. Levine-Clark, *Unemployment, Welfare and Masculine Citizenship: So Much Honest Poverty in Britain 1870–1930* (Basingstoke, 2015).

107. On continuity and change in the positions of Victorian poverty experts, see Martin, *Hard and Unreal Advice*, while for changing thinking in the philanthropic community see Ginn, *Culture, Philanthropy*. Hennock, 'The measurement', provides a compelling description of differences of method and interpretation amongst social investigators in London and the provinces. See also M. Brodie, *The Politics of the Poor: The East End of London, 1885–1914* (Oxford, 2004).

108. D Englander, *Poverty and Poor Law Reform in Nineteenth-Century Britain, 1834–1914* (London, 1998), 1.

109. This process is clearly visible in the correspondence between Boards of Guardians and the central authorities in London. See P. Carter and S. King, 'Keeping Track: Modern Methods, Administration and the Victorian Poor Law, 1834–1871', *Archives*, 60 (2014), 31–52.

110. See, for example, W. Cunningham Glen, *The General Consolidated Order Issued by the Poor Law Commissioners* (London, 1847); *The General Consolidated and other Orders of the Poor Law Guardians and the Poor Law Board* (6th ed., London, 1868); *The General Orders of the Poor Law Commissioners, the Poor Law Board, and the Local Government Board Relating to the Poor Law* (London, 1898). For an overview of this publication process see Frankel, *States of Inquiry*.

111. For example, William Golden Lumley, who was himself Assistant Secretary to the Poor Law Board, published multiple editions of his guide, *The Master and Matron of the Workhouse* (2nd ed., London 1869).

CHAPTER 2

Not That Joseph Rowntree: The Amateur Workhouse Inspector

Abstract Our second chapter begins to address the question of how a more focussed workhouse reform movement grew and gained traction. We concentrate in particular on the role of amateur social investigators and the part that they played in informing, shaping and, in some cases, creating public opinion on the need for workhouse reform. For the very first time in the historiography of the New Poor Law, we address the workhouse investigation programme of Joseph Rowntree. Very likely a close relative of the more famous Victorian philanthropist, Rowntree traversed the length and breadth of England and Wales (as well making forays into Scotland and Ireland) gaining access to workhouses and reporting through letters to the press on the conditions he found and the reforms he felt were needed. Sometimes, notably in relation to the casual poor, observation turned to action in individual cases as Rowntree sought to use the laws, rules and regulations of the New Poor Law to hold individual officers and Unions to account. For his pains, he was attacked in print by many local interest groups who sought to portray him as a meddling amateur and tried to rebut his criticisms of individual places and practices. But Rowntree went further than this, corresponding on his findings with the various incarnations of the central authorities whose job it was to oversee and control local practice. This simultaneous engagement on the local and national stages means that Rowntree's neglect in the existing literature is surprising and his revival in this book all the more important for an understanding of the nature and pace of workhouse reform sentiment.

© The Author(s) 2020   39
P. Jones, S. King, *Pauper Voices, Public Opinion and Workhouse Reform in Mid-Victorian England*,
https://doi.org/10.1007/978-3-030-47839-1_2

INTRODUCTION

As we began to suggest in the last chapter, the period after 1850 witnessed the increasing presence of poverty experts, literary and other authors, editors, social workers, cultural and material philanthropists and social investigators in press coverage of the New Poor Law. Their collective diagnosis of the scale and causes of poverty, the degree of personal responsibility for need, and the suitability of outdoor relief and the workhouse for its amelioration, varied across a wide spectrum. Such variation, mirrored as it was in the political sphere of this period, meant that nothing approaching a comprehensive and systematic plan for reform of the New Poor Law or its workhouses was to gain traction before the early 1900s.[1] Nonetheless, knowledge of the poor in both a theoretical and a practical sense deepened in this period, and investigatory imperatives and methods pioneered in London percolated throughout the country. In turn, the scale of interest in poverty and poor relief seems to have created a public receptive to the views and publicity of a growing cadre of amateur but authoritative figures who sought to make their mark on understandings of later nineteenth-century social conditions. Sometimes this became a family affair, as it did in the case of the Rowntrees of Yorkshire.

Many readers will be familiar with Joseph Rowntree, Quaker, philanthropist and the man behind one of the best-known confectionary firms in the world. Even if they know few details about his life, many more will have come across his name through the work of the three foundations he endowed and that continue his work in modified form.[2] Rowntree's main philanthropic concerns were, first, to establish the means to investigate the deep roots of poverty in Britain, and second, to find lasting ways to alleviate it. As he wrote in a now-famous memorandum, "I feel that much of the current philanthropic effort is directed to remedying the more superficial manifestations of weakness or evil, while little thought is directed to search out their underlying causes".[3] Joseph's work and underlying vision inspired his son, Seebohm, to undertake a now classic survey of the living conditions of the poor in York at the end of the nineteenth century. Joseph's continued influence and endowments mark him out as a truly remarkable figure, a trailblazer in the field of modern social inquiry.[4] It comes as something of a surprise, then, to discover that he was not the only Joseph Rowntree who used his time and resources to serve the mid-Victorian poor in this way, highlighting their plight and advocating for social reform on their behalf. In fact, he was not even the only philanthropic Joseph

Rowntree from Yorkshire. This chapter looks in detail at another, less well-known but nonetheless active J. Rowntree. He lived in Leeds and, between 1859 and at least 1868, travelled the length and breadth of mainland Britain visiting workhouses, and sometimes jails, on a mission to uncover and expose the truth about the conditions of the institutionalised poor and, in particular, about how indoor relief was administered.

As we shall see, his philanthropic work was, in substance (and not unexpectedly given the rich seam of amateur activity in this area traced above and in Chap. 1), related to that of other unofficial workhouse visitors, although he himself does not appear to have identified with any wider visiting or reform "'movement", such as Louisa Twining's Workhouse Visiting Society. But his actions also provide us with a vital empirical bridge between those other reforming currents and the great organs of mid-Victorian public opinion because this Joseph Rowntree faithfully, almost obsessively, reported his findings in the local press at all the locations he visited, and he also entered into lengthy correspondence with the Poor Law Board in London on issues of particular concern. In the course of researching this chapter, we have uncovered more than 150 letters and opinion pieces written either by him or in response to his observations published in 47 different newspapers and periodicals across the United Kingdom, from Stonehaven to Somerset and from Bedford to Belfast (Table 2.1).[5] Like his namesake, this Joseph Rowntree was also part of the Yorkshire Quaker community and it is clear that his work was similarly rooted in the Friends' long tradition of social duty and personal obligation. He seems to have been an orthodox member of his religious community: he used the by-then fast waning Quaker forms of address in his personal correspondence—the "thees" and "thous" that often drew ridicule from contemporaries—and he dated his letters according to the number of the month rather than using the pagan names. Indeed, it is almost certain that there was a connection between him and the York Rowntrees, perhaps even a close family connection—we know, for example, that both Josephs had personal links to Scarborough in North Yorkshire—but unfortunately there is nothing in his writings or in the available genealogical archives that allows us to pin down the exact nature of that relationship.

As we have noted, at no point in his voluminous correspondence did this Joseph Rowntree attempt to ally himself with any of the other more high profile groups and individuals who were carrying out similar work, particularly in the capital, and neither did he try to build his investigations

Table 2.1   Newspaper and journal titles in which Joseph Rowntree is known to have had letters published between 1859 and 1868

Bedfordshire Mercury	Knaresborough Post	Nottingham Guardian
Belfast Newsletter	Leeds Intelligencer	Preston Chronicle
Blackburn Standard	Leeds Mercury	Rochdale Observer
Bradford Observer	Leeds Times	Sheffield & Rotherham Independent
Bury Times	Leicester Chronicle	Sheffield and Rotherham Independent
Cardiff & Merthyr Guardian	Liverpool Mercury	Sheffield Daily Telegraph
Cardiff Times	London City Press	Somerset County Gazette
Carlisle Journal	Manchester Courier	Stonehaven Journal
Carmarthen Reporter	Manchester Times	The British Friend
Cheshire Observer	Merthyr Telegraph	The Poor Law Magazine
Dundee, Perth & Cupar Advertiser	Newcastle Daily Mail	Western Times
Durham County Advertiser	Newcastle Guardian	Wrexham Advertiser
Gloucester Journal	North & South Shields Gazette	York Gazette
Hereford Times	North Wales Chronicle	York Herald
Hertfordshire Express	Northampton Mercury	Yorkshire Post
Huddersfield Chronicle	Nottingham Daily Express	

Source: British Library Newspaper Collections Online (https://www.britishnewspaperarchive.co.uk/)

and advocacy into anything like an organised campaign. Instead, he seems to have been content to let his observations speak for themselves, and to trust in the integrity of his investigations and the power of the press to shape and influence public opinion. His dedication is beyond doubt and Rowntree's actions must have cost him a great deal in terms of time, energy and personal expense.[6] Yet he sought little obvious reward beyond the satisfaction of following his conscience and advocating for those less fortunate than himself. But, as we argue below, despite the quiet and largely unheralded manner in which he undertook his missions on behalf of the poor, and the fact that he has so far remained anonymous to posterity, this "other" Joseph Rowntree undertook work of genuine importance in the history of workhouse reform. Nonetheless, his work can only be understood within the context of the wider reform movement that this book seeks to describe, a series of currents and trends which, though discrete, flowed together to influence public opinion and to bring about changes in the administration of indoor relief and the experience of workhouse inmates. There is no doubt that Rowntree's investigative work was influenced by many of these other currents, and by wider fields of social investigation into orphan children, the housing of the poor and the nature of wages in urban Britain.[7] Equally, however, there is no question that, given the scale of his published correspondence and the reach of his work-house visits, he was in turn a significant influence on this diffuse reform movement, and his work is one such current in and of itself.

THE AMATEUR WORKHOUSE INSPECTOR

As we noted above, it is possible for the period 1859–1868 to find at least 150 letters written by, or about, Rowntree which appeared in the local press for England, Wales, Scotland and Ireland. Yet, these letters were actually the mid- or end-point of his investigative process. As we read the corpus, it becomes clear that Rowntree developed a routine for gaining access to, and reporting on, the workhouses he visited. His developing strategy is already in evidence in the first of his rediscovered letters, pub-lished in the *Liverpool Mercury* on 11 November 1859. In it, he explained that he had been "invited to accompany three Liverpool gentlemen (one of them being the chairman of the board [of guardians])", to inspect the Liverpool workhouse as an impartial observer. This clause relating to his impartiality was revisited at the end of the letter, when he insisted that "I am an entire stranger to all contractors and officials, and it is alone on the score of humanity and *justice*, as a Christian man, I now press on your seri-ous attention the foregoing comments".[8] It was something that he restated many times in his subsequent correspondence and has sustained resonance in wider concepts of Christian philanthropy stretching back to the Old Poor Law and beyond.

Although there is nothing in this letter to indicate a close personal rela-tionship with any of the guardians who invited him to visit the workhouse, it is notable that the man who Rowntree believed to be chairman of the board (mistakenly, as it turned out) was James Cropper.[9] Cropper was a paper merchant (1823–1900), a noted philanthropist himself, and a slav-ery abolitionist known locally as "The most generous man in Liverpool".[10] Crucially, Cropper, though a recent convert to the Church of England, was from strong Lancashire Quaker stock: his father was a Quaker-merchant and his grandfather, also James (1773–1840), was the first merchant-philanthropist of his line and was himself a well-known aboli-tionist.[11] Indeed, Rowntree notes this lineage in his letter, writing that it was a worthy thing for "a descendant of the honoured philanthropist and skilful deviser for the poor and outcast" to use his influence to improve the lot of the Liverpool poor.[12] It is therefore very likely that Rowntree used his connections within the tight-knit northern Quaker community to gain access to the Liverpool workhouse, and perhaps to others as well. This is important, for as a private individual and an "unauthorised visitor", Rowntree sometimes faced difficulties in gaining entry to workhouses, something noted by other philanthropic workhouse visitors. Louisa Twining, for example, felt that it was of the utmost importance to "open the 'closed doors' of the workhouse", believing that this would "make mismanagement and cruel treatment of the poor less likely".[13] Rowntree's difficulties were exacerbated as he published more accounts of his visits and as his notoriety as a critic of workhouse regimes spread. For example, having once visited the Newcastle workhouse in January 1862, Rowntree was subsequently rebuffed by the guardians when he reapplied later that month, despite having a recommendation from the Mayor of Tynemouth. The curt reply to his second application was that the guardians were "fully competent to manage the workhouse … without his assistance".[14] We will move on to discuss the reception of Rowntree's observations at some length later in the chapter, but it is clear from this and other evidence that although he faced opposition to his visits, Rowntree was able to muster considerable resources to allow him to gain access to workhouses as a private individual including, it is likely, a network of philanthropic connections from whom he was able to gain recommendations.

Returning to that first letter about the conditions he found at Liverpool in 1859, Rowntree was at first keen to give credit where it was due, observing that "The general good management and thorough cleanliness of this large establishment are apparent"; but thereafter he wrote a long and damning report on the practice of setting female paupers to grind corn at a flour mill. Not only was the resulting flour of poor quality, he maintained, but the cruelty of the practice and the poor conditions endured by the women were unconscionable: "They work in long narrow passages", he wrote, which were "walled up on each side and at the far end, and are very badly ventilated… During the summer and warmer weather it is an outrage on humanity to see the perspiration running down the poor women, who are kept grinding at once the tough bad wheat and their own lives".[15] It is clear from this and subsequent letters to the *Mercury* that he was particularly perturbed by the use of the corn mill as a labour test for paupers, noting that it was quite literally a case of "grinding the faces of the poor", and asking: "[are these] 'the rights of women' in your town, which is rapidly advancing in reform of every character"?[16] Indeed, it is likely that what he found at Liverpool was a stimulus for his later intensive investigations, at least in part. Yet it is obvious from his next letter to the *Mercury* that Rowntree's interest in workhouses had deeper roots. On 3 December, in response to criticism of his first letter by the Liverpool Board of Guardians, Rowntree wrote that: "I was in Ireland 17 weeks during the famine, and visited a large number of the unions, reporting on them to the Poor Law Board in Dublin entirely at my own cost. My progress was stopped, from being attacked with the typhus fever". He went on to assure his readers that "I do not name this from egotism, but to show that I know something of what union houses should be".[17]

Details of his next recorded workhouse visits are given in a letter published in the *Bury Times* in January 1860, and relate to the Bury and Haslingden unions. The tone of this letter is subtly different to the ones regarding Liverpool. Already, at this early stage of his published investigations, Rowntree seems to have shifted his focus away from uncovering gross abuses and cruelties and towards a more general critique of the way that workhouses were run on a day-to-day basis. Of Bury, he wrote that, although it was a new workhouse with a master who "understands his business, and endeavours to carry out the instructions of the guardians", it was nonetheless systemically deficient. There was a lack of paid nurses for the "excitable" women, for example, and the doctor only visited twice a week rather than once a day, which Rowntree suggested was essential. In addition, he highlighted a lack of instruction for younger, short-term inmates (most of the longer-term children were sent away to the Swinton School in Manchester) and the neglect of useful instruction for adult paupers, such as mat-making or industrial training. Of Haslingden, he commented that, though an old building, it was kept clean and "some case exists in regard to ventilation". Once again, though, he lamented inadequate instruction of children and went on to note a number of other concerns, such as the lack of activities for elderly and infirm inmates, and the paucity of suitable reading matter (by which he meant scriptural texts) and reading glasses.[18]

As we have noted, the tone of this second letter was more procedural than the first. Rather than a preoccupation with specific examples of workhouse cruelty, which tend to characterise newspaper correspondence and reportage relating to workhouses in the early- to mid-nineteenth century, as we saw in Chap. 1, this letter reads much more like the report of a formal inspection. Indeed, Rowntree himself clearly conceived of his role in that way, noting that "I have had the opportunity of inspecting the workhouses and schools" of Bury and Haslingden.[19] It is also clear from this and subsequent correspondence that these visits were part of a much broader investigation into "various [workhouses] of Lancashire", including those at Blackburn, Rochdale, Preston, Wigan, Hollingsworth, Penwortham, Walton, Bamber Bridge and Ribchester.[20] This focus is perhaps unsurprising. The faults of the New Poor Law system—its unsuitability for areas where cyclical industry or structural decline predominated; uncertainty over how to deal with illegitimacy in areas of high incidence; the problem of what to do with aged men; and the unsuitability of workhouses for child welfare, for instance—were likely to have been writ large in the county and would have been predictable to the amateur observer. Moreover, outside of the metropolis, Lancashire clearly had the largest concentration of large urban workhouses within easy travelling distance of each other.[21] Rowntree's reports on these workhouses conform very closely to the pattern set at Bury and Haslingden, and he again described his visits as "inspections". He was particularly damning of Preston workhouse which, with its poor ventilation, overcrowding, dirty and insanitary conditions and "deplorable" hospital, led him to conclude that "The only remedy is a new workhouse, combining all the needful appendages, such as hospital, workshops, school-rooms of a suitable area, [and] a bakehouse".[22] As this observation makes clear, Rowntree was not against workhouses per se. Instead, his concerns were that in many cases they were poorly run and, on occasion, unfit-for-purpose. This is important, because it helps us to understand not only Rowntree's preoccupations as an amateur workhouse inspector, but the context within which he undertook his labours. As we saw in Chap. 1, beyond the anti-New Poor Law sentiment of radicals and Tories in the years following the passing of the PLAA, there was very little appetite for a complete dismantling of the "workhouse system"; but this is very different from suggesting that the mid-Victorian populace was comfortable either with the nature of the deterrent mixed workhouse, or with the ways in which individual institutions were run. In turn, exposés like Rowntree's were central to the creation and maintenance of an influential body of popular opinion that applied pressure locally (on Boards of Guardians) and nationally (on the Poor Law Board), to ensure that officials adhered to the rules and fulfilled their duty of care to indoor paupers.[23]

In this context, Rowntree asked the question: "how is it that Preston ladies do not form a committee for weekly visiting the various workhouses

and schools?"[24] This particular concern—the need for ladies' visiting committees—is, of course, resonant of (and, indeed, directly attributable to)
the efforts of Louisa Twining and other important women philanthropists
in the 1850s and 1860s, and it is something to which we will return
shortly. But at this stage, it is important to note that it was a common
thread in much of his correspondence, part of a raft of preoccupations
which, taken together, might be described as a manifesto for good workhouse governance that Rowntree developed and promoted throughout
the remainder of his newspaper correspondence. As we have seen, other
recurring themes in this putative manifesto related to proper ventilation;
paid nursing and care staff, particularly on the hospital wards; more regular and diligent professional medical attendance; the provision of industrial
training for inmates; and better attention to spiritual well-being. During
the period of his most intense letter-writing activity, Rowntree presented
this "manifesto" many times in provincial newspapers as a stand-alone
document, not specifically connected to any particular workhouse but as a
series of observations and recommendations on better institutional governance overall.[25] The first of these general letters was published in the
Sheffield and Rotherham Independent in December 1861, and thereafter it
appeared, in modified form, in the *North and South Shields Gazette*, the
York Gazette, the *Northampton Mercury*, the *Hertfordshire Express*, the
Bedfordshire Mercury and other local publications between 1861 and
1867. This sort of activity was underpinned by a wider ongoing canvas of
investigation. In other letters, Rowntree continued to discuss these preoccupations and concerns with specific reference to the many other workhouses he visited (Table 2.2). Indeed, as his correspondence unfolded,
only one other major concern relating to workhouse administration seems
to have been added to this early list of grievances, and that related to the
treatment of vagrants/casual paupers, a theme to which we now turn.

ROWNTREE AND THE CASUAL POOR

The issue of "casuals" or vagrants[26] was one that generated considerable
debate and consternation under the New Poor Law, just as it had under
the Old.[27] While there are many problems with defining who was encap-
sulated by the label "vagrant", most historians concur that the nineteenth
century saw a steady and at times rapid increase in their numbers. This
reflected better systems of surveillance and apprehension on the one hand,
but also growing urbanisation, the so-called flight from the countryside,

Table 2.2 Workhouses and workhouse institutions known to have been visited by Joseph Rowntree between 1859 and 1868

England				Wales	Scotland (Poorhouses)	Ireland
Alston with Garrigill	Gloucester	Liverpool	Rochdale	Bala	Dundee	Dublin
Birkby (Huddersfield)	Halifax	Macclesfield	Rotherham	Bedwelty	Edinburgh	Belfast
Birkenhead	Haltwhistle	New Bridge Street (Manchester)	Sheffield	Brecknock	Glasgow	
Blackburn	Haslingden	Marylebone	South Shields	Cardiff	Stonehaven	
Bradford	Hartismere	Middlesborough	Stockton	Carmarthen	Wigtown	
Bury	Hay	Newcastle	Sunderland	Corwen		
Carlisle	Holborn	North Shields (Tynemouth)	Toxteth Park	Dolgellau		
Chester	Hollingsworth	Nottingham	Walton-le-Dale Workhouse School (Bamber Bridge)	Montgomery & Welshpool		
Crumpsall (Manchester)	Huddersfield	Otley	Wardleworth (Rochdale)	Neath		
Darlington	Knaresborough	Penwortham Workhouse School (Preston)	Warrington	Wrexham		
Deanhouses	Lambeth	Prescot	Wellington			
Derby	Leeds	Preston	Wigan			
Eccleshall Bierlow	Leicester	Ribchester				

Source: British Library Newspaper Collections Online (https://www.britishnewspaperarchive.co.uk/)

agricultural depression and the growing casualization of jobs in some areas.[28] Certainly, by the 1850s, a censorious discussion (and associated episodic moral panics) was emerging that viewed vagrants and casuals as a particular breeding ground for the "contagion" of immorality and demoralisation among the poor.[29] Even though much of the contemporary literature focused (as it continues to do) on the metropolis, it was an issue which exercised contemporaries across England and Wales. One journal, aimed at poor law administrators and justices of the peace, for example, noted as early 1848 that "[t]here is hardly a county in England from which we have not received one or more letters representing the heavy burden which falls upon particular parishes by reason of the great increase in the number of the wandering poor".[30] Since the passing of the Vagrancy Act in 1824, the vagrant and tramping poor were liable to be sentenced to hard labour if they were found sleeping in the open.[31] Under the new regime, one solution was to build dedicated "casual wards" in workhouses, barely adequate sleeping accommodation where those who had no other refuge could be accommodated for short periods (usually a single night at a time). The problem for local Boards of Guardians and the central authorities was one of deterrence: it was important to ensure that sufficient accommodation was provided for casuals to prevent them sleeping rough, but it was equally imperative that it should be harsh enough not to encourage vagrancy and the licentious lifestyle of the unattached "tramp".[32] Crowther suggests that by the 1860s, "a "theory of casuals began to develop" which, though "confused" and incomplete, nonetheless stimulated a different approach to their welfare and supervision.[33] The result was, first, the Metropolitan Houseless Poor Act of 1864. This provided central funds for increased casual accommodation in London's workhouses and required the police to direct tramps and vagrants towards them. The act was followed in 1871 by the Pauper Inmates Discharge and Regulation Act, which allowed for the detention of casual paupers until they had fulfilled a stated quantity of work in return for their board and lodging.[34] The central plank of these two pieces of legislation (strengthened by the Casual Poor Act of 1882) was that "labour became compulsory" for casuals (particularly men), and that such labour should be "suitably deterrent".[35] It is against this backdrop that social workers, poverty experts and social investigators took on the work of exploring vagrancy.

Rowntree first raised the issue of the casual poor in May 1862, in a letter to the *Northampton Mercury*.[36] In particular, he highlighted the uneven treatment of "casuals" across England, complaining that there was "great irregularity" between workhouses and that "The standing orders of the Poor-Law Board in respect to this class of paupers are not complied with in very many unions".[37] He went on to provide specific examples from his own observations in the north and north-east of England, insisting that guardians and workhouse officials had a responsibility "to carry out the regulation for relieving the destitute casual poor with *food* and *lodging*", observing that "[in] some other towns the amount of work required before food is given is frequently unwarrantable".[38] Later, he expanded on these observations, noting that:

> By the law of England it is provided that every poor person in a state of destitution shall receive relief from a public fund, in food, in clothing, in lodging, or in medical or surgical assistance, according to the needs of such person. No question is raised as to the [*illegible word*], sex, age, *character, or conduct of the destitute*. The only inquiry is as to the *actual destitution*.[39]

Rowntree went further in subsequent letters and, by the mid-1860s, the treatment of casuals and vagrants seems to have become a particular preoccupation for him, as it had for the press more widely.[40] In 1866, for example, he published another letter in the *Liverpool Mercury* on the subject of "English Workhouses and Night Asylums" (another name for casual wards) which appears to have been the result of further concentrated enquiries made by him in the greater Liverpool region. In it, he described the treatment of casual paupers at Birkenhead, Warrington, Wigan, Prescot, Macclesfield and Chester. He made a number of important observations, including: inadequate heating and bedding in most of the casual wards he visited, poor diet, and that casuals were often set to hard labour (such as stone-breaking) early in the morning before being given anything to eat which, he wrote, was unconscionable given that many of them had eaten little or nothing on the previous day.[41] For Macclesfield, Rowntree reported that paupers described the casual wards as "amongst the worst in the country... It is scarcely possible to conceive of greater omissions of the requirements of the law and the dictates of humanity than is practised at Macclesfield casual wards". For Birkenhead he made another telling observation: that casuals were expected to bathe in water which had already been used many times over, leading him to exclaim that "Men and women even in the lowest depths of poverty have human feelings, which ought not to be outraged in this way".[42] Collectively, these observations (which mirror those coming out of literary texts and first-hand testimony from those who managed to get inside casual wards) signal an important division in Victorian society between those who viewed vagrants with open compassion and a wider public view that constructed vagrants as dangerous, disruptive and dishonest and as a group that needed to be discouraged, and even punished, to the full extent of the law.[43]

This sense that Rowntree had sympathy with the vagrant situation is magnified by the fact that he occasionally strayed beyond his usual role as an unofficial inspector of workhouses, taking direct action on behalf of individuals who he considered had been treated particularly badly. In 1863, for example, he reported on the plight of a young woman, Hannah Kendrew, who had been forced by ill-health to quit her job in West Lutton, a small village in Ryedale, North Yorkshire. Kendrew had, he reported, been told by the relieving officer to return to her own parish, which she believed to be Leeds, and accordingly she set out to walk the fifty miles to get there. Having arrived at York, she was taken into the workhouse as a vagrant and given a single night's lodging; but, Rowntree reported, she had been allowed no food and been required to move on in the morning. Kendrew told him that she had received the same treatment at Tadcaster workhouse, and that her only sustenance on the fifty mile trek was a cup of tea and a morsel of bread from another poor woman.[44] Having finally arrived at Leeds, Kendrew was then told by a relieving officer, under the direction of the Board of Guardians, that she was no longer the responsibility of the Leeds Poor Law Union because she had subsequently gained a settlement through service in West Lutton.[45] As a result, she was allowed to remain a single night in the workhouse as a vagrant and then told to find her own way back to Malton, the nearest town to Lutton. All she was given to eat at the Leeds workhouse, she said, was another piece of dry bread and nothing at all to drink. According to Rowntree, it was then that he met her, "a poor woman in scant attire, with a way-worn countenance", and she told him her story.[46]

Rowntree's response to Kendrew's plight is illuminating. Eschewing the outrage he may have felt at her treatment, Rowntree instead wrote in measured terms about the legality of the various officials' actions. In the first place, he questioned publicly whether the Leeds guardians had the right to treat her as a vagrant, regardless of the details of her settlement. "Kendrew knows that she was born in Leeds", he wrote, "and from ill health is turned out of her situation, and is induced to walk fifty miles in search of a workhouse home", where she was "summarily dealt with and dismissed". But, he concluded, because she honestly believed Leeds to be her place of settlement, "[s]he cannot be designated a vagrant".[47] Rowntree also queried the behaviour of the Malton guardians, who told Kendrew to make her own way to Leeds despite the fact that she was recovering from illness. In the case of a sick pauper, he pointed out, the nearest Board of Guardians was legally bound to relieve her, and she could not be sent to her parish of settlement until she was fully recovered. This was an accurate depiction of the law and practice of the New Poor Law at this date. Finally, Rowntree aimed his pen at the officials in York, asking whether the ratepayers "are satisfied with the York Guardians systematically evading the standing legal regulation under the Poor Law Act in not giving their casual poor, or even what are improperly termed vagrants, the '8 oz. of bread night and morning, as required by the above act'".[48] Rooted in Christian philanthropy, Rowntree's actions in this case locate him on the same canvas as other Victorian poverty experts, though clearly less censorious than some of those with a higher public and governmental profile.[49]

Kendrew's was not an isolated act of advocacy on behalf of the casual poor as far as Rowntree was concerned. In 1866, for example, he took up the case of Thomas Burke who, it was alleged, had been assaulted by the porter of the Manchester workhouse at Crumpsall. The first account of Rowntree's involvement was not, this time, from his own hand. Rather, it appeared in a newspaper report from the *Manchester Courier* of the trial which ensued against the porter, Francis Dalton. According to the report, Burke had applied for admission to the Crumpsall workhouse for a night's shelter, having nowhere else to go, and Dalton had told him that he would have to grind corn for his keep.[50] Burke insisted he could not do so because of a bad leg, and asked that he should be taken to the workhouse doctor to prove the fact. Dalton's response was to drag him up the workhouse steps and throw him into the street, slamming the door in his face. It was then that Rowntree came across Burke and, hearing his story, knocked at the workhouse door.[51] In the exchange that followed, Rowntree again raised the issue of the regulations issued by the Poor Law Board, insisting that Burke must be admitted, having no other lodgings and having had no food that day. Dalton at first refused, insisting that Burke could not stay in the workhouse unless he worked for his keep. Eventually Rowntree persuaded Dalton to take Burke to see the workhouse doctor who confirmed that he was unfit for work, and he was allowed to stay the night and receive his allocation of bread for supper and breakfast. The following day, however, Rowntree was again waiting for him outside the workhouse, and this time he persuaded Burke to take his complaint to the magistrates.[52]

While the pretext for Rowntree's involvement in Burke's case was the assault by Dalton, it becomes clear in the *Courier's* report of the trial that there was far more to it than that. In their testimony, other pauper witnesses stated that they had been kept waiting for admission to the casual ward for upwards of four hours in a cold, unheated passageway, and that they were only attended to after midnight. On being questioned by the magistrate, Rowntree freely admitted that he was only a witness to Burke's treatment because he had been watching the workhouse to gather information about the treatment of casual paupers more generally. He, too, affirmed that many of them had told him they were forced to wait for hours in the freezing cold and that they were not given food or any kind of covering until after midnight. He was also told that up to six casuals were forced to share the same bath water on entering the night asylum. Returning to Burke, Rowntree stated that his only object in intervening in his case was "to be a witness for the man", and that "this was a most important part of an Englishman's duty, as many a man was trodden under foot for the want of a witness".[53] This, in itself, tells us a great deal about Rowntree's motivations as an amateur workhouse "inspector" and advocate for the vagrant poor; and, of course, it speaks vividly to his obligations as an active Quaker.[54] Whether he orchestrated the charges against Dalton simply to engineer a public platform for his concerns, or whether, having gained that platform, he raised them opportunistically, it is impossible to say for certain. But the end result was that the presiding magistrate, Mr. Fowler, agreed with him that there were many issues at the Manchester workhouse which required further investigation. In summing up after the first day of the trial, Fowler stated that:

> though this was a charge of common assault, it was in reality a public inquiry of a very serious description. It was that which ought not to be decided by any magistrates merely upon a charge of common assault. No doubt the case would be made public through the channel of the press, and if it were not, he would take good care that the authorities were furnished with a full note of what transpired. He was quite sure such inquiry would be made into the case as it certainly deserved.[55]

In order to allow for a full official inquiry into the allegations made by Rowntree and the casual paupers who gave evidence at Burke's trial, the magistrate then adjourned the summons against Dalton for a full month. Rowntree, however, left nothing to chance and his subsequent actions highlight one mechanism by which the central authorities of the New Poor Law were alerted to public sentiment but also suggest the power of public opinion in shaping local and national practice.

ROWNTREE AND THE POOR LAW BOARD

The day after the above report appeared in the *Manchester Courier*, Rowntree wrote to the Poor Law Board to alert them to the proceedings at Dalton's trial.[56] Over the next two months, he wrote a further twenty letters direct to the Board about the situation in Manchester, totalling almost 30,000 words.[57] Whilst Dalton's case was the pretext for opening this correspondence, Rowntree soon strayed far beyond it, making it his business to report on the situation across Manchester's poor law institutions in minute detail. He gave the circumstances of many individual cases of harsh treatment, often transcribing letters from paupers themselves which he included with his own in order to corroborate his evidence. Despite these detailed case studies, and his advocacy on behalf of individual paupers, it is clear that his overarching purpose was to provide a general critique of the way that Manchester's workhouses were being run. In his first letter, he wrote that "I have notes in my pocket touching on many irregularities that I fear have been going on at various establishments immediatly [sic] under the charge of the Manchester Board of Guardians".[58] He first confined himself to the situation at the Night Asylum, but by April 1866 he had turned his attention to the hospital wards in the old workhouse at Bridge Street, and particularly the fever ward. It was, he wrote, woefully understaffed with only one paid nurse in attendance, a Mrs. Thornton, who "worked beyond her strength" and performed the duties "which ought to have devolved upon at least three paid women". On the evidence of a female pauper assistant to Thornton, Rowntree reported that the nurse finally succumbed to the strain of her exertions, dying of typhus exacerbated by exhaustion. "Thus", he concluded, "the mainspring of the fever hospital was finally severed". Rowntree had no hesitation in placing the responsibility for Thornton's death with the guardians, who "never appear to have manifested any adequate sense of their obligations towards such a valuable public servant".[59] Thereafter, he dedicated the remaining ten sides of this closely written letter to the further failings of the Guardians and officials on the fever wards at Bridge Street.[60]

In subsequent letters, he accused the Master of the same workhouse of interfering in the care of the sick poor, in direct contravention of the workhouse surgeon's instructions, and of petty tyrannies over the elderly and infirm; he took aim at the diet of the poor, particularly the sick poor, accusing the guardians of changing it for the worse without consulting the Poor Law Board (something they were required to do), and of substituting suet pudding for a potato hash which "it would puzzle a pelican to digest". He even reported, "on undoubted authority", that the house surgeon at Bridge Street had resigned in protest at the reduction of the rations for the sick poor.[61] The following month, he complained that "many of the abuses first complained of" at the Crumpsall workhouse, "still flourish as rank and luxuriously as ever", and once again he gave details of a number of individual case studies to support his assertion.[62] In his final letter to the Poor Law Board about Manchester, Rowntree revisited his particular concern about the use of corn mills as a form of labour for inmates. At Crumpsall, he wrote, "6 ½ pecks of Corn [are] required to be ground there as a days work", which was, he wrote, "above the prison quantity of labour".[63] He described it as "a great national question", and appealed directly:

> to the President of the Poor Law Board to fully investigate the matter—and to ascertain whether or no it be the fact, that more hard labour is demanded in workhouses than prisons … [and] whether an equal quantity of food is given to support men performing such hard labour in our workhouses with our prisons—Many believe the balance is greatly in favour of the latter.[64]

Indeed, most of the content of Rowntree's correspondence to the Poor Law Board on the subject of the Manchester union can be read as a plea for them to investigate the situation there thoroughly and conscientiously. He claimed that this correspondence "contained a mass of incontrovertible facts, founded on evidence which I believe would have satisfied any English judge, or any enlightened and impartial jury".[65] Still, he found the Board slow to act, and, in particular, he considered its own (paid) inspectors inadequate to the task of exposing and addressing instances of neglect and wrongdoing. In 1862, relatively early in his investigative work, Rowntree had stated that "[t]he visits of the Poor-Law Board Inspectors should be more frequent: and more time should be devoted to the thorough scrutiny of every department, in order that it may be ascertained how each paid officer is discharging his or her individual duty".[66] Shortly after the publication of this observation, the first real fault lines between Rowntree and the official inspectorate began to emerge. On visiting workhouses in and around Carlisle, he wrote that "the necessity for my giving publicity to my observations has increased", because of the infrequency of the official inspector's visits. However, he also revealed that the inspector had "objected to my being allowed to enter my observations in the visitors' book, on account of my not holding any official position".[67] By the time of his correspondence with the Poor Law Board in 1866, he had come to the conclusion that "I do not think the Inspectors from the Poor law Board sufficiently investigate [such] matters", and he expressly asked that an inspector's visit to Manchester:

> be made in the presence of reporters of the press as the high opinion he entertains of the Guardians and officials greatly impairs his powers of taking a correct and impartial view of the serious cases I have submitted to your Board for the public good & the welfare of the poor.[68]

Rowntree maintained that inspectors were easily deceived, not least because they only visited sporadically, and then by appointment. "It is not to be expected", he wrote, "that the officers in workhouses will break the law and set aside the regulations before an inspector's eyes". Citing a number of cases where misconduct and cruelty had been exposed as a result of complaints by members of the public and paupers themselves, he asked: "Where should we have been, if outsiders had not brought to light gross abuses, which official inspection failed to detect"?[69] Nonetheless, despite his reservations about the official inspectors, and notwithstanding his own exhaustive efforts to highlight wrongdoing and bad management, he still maintained that "It should certainly not be left to unpaid volunteers to discover and report the *great abuses* which exist", and that the real work of investigation was "the Inspectors' duty".[70]

Rowntree's mounting concern about the deficiencies in the inspection and oversight of workhouse officials finds a close parallel in the complaints of paupers themselves to the Poor Law Board. This is something that will be explored in much more detail in Chap. 3. Meanwhile, it is clear from his correspondence with the Board, along with the extensive record of his letters to the press, that Rowntree felt obliged to "bear witness" on behalf of the workhouse poor because of what he saw as the failure of guardians and officials to observe the rules laid down by the Board, and to crack down on specific abuses and systematic failings in workhouse administration. Thus, he explicitly hoped that the inspector's investigations at Manchester would be done in the presence of reporters, to ensure transparency and proper public scrutiny of the process. Much earlier, in 1860, in response to the criticisms of the Leeds Board of Guardians regarding one of his published letters, he stated that he had many times complained to them about various aspects of workhouse life, such as the lack of education for poor children and (once again) the injurious use of corn grinding mills as a form of employment. But, he wrote, "I found no disposition to give my views any consideration" and, as a result:

> I have found the public press a far better medium to the ratepayers than, after devoting many months to inspecting workhouses, to leave all the facts to be dealt with by Guardians. I have tested each mode, and find the press and the ratepayers of this country far more influential than Boards of Guardians.[71]

There were occasions on which this sort of intervention with centre and locality achieved tangible results in terms of the abuses he sought to highlight. At Rochdale, for example, his published criticisms of the Master and the Medical Officer in relation to the treatment of a "weak minded" pauper who had been kept locked in the vagrant's ward for many days "without fire or sufficient clothes", stimulated an inquiry by the Board's inspectors, and eventually resulted in the censure of the two officials.[72] Successes like this provide support for the idea that the centre in particular was sensitive to the potential impact of sustained negative publicity, an observation that does much to connect Rowntree with the wider currents of workhouse criticism analysed in Chap. 1.[73] There we suggested that while those who commented on the deterrent workhouse did so across a wide philosophical, moral and sentimental spectrum, almost all criticisms were of how the system was run, managed and inspected rather than amounting to an organised argument for repeal and replacement of the New Poor Law. In this sense, Rowntree's writing was perhaps more visceral, highly charged and favourable to the emerging sense that poverty may not have been the fault of the individual, than was the case with other social investigators, philanthropists and social workers working around the same time, but he was still seeking to work within the limits of the system. On the other hand, Rowntree's remarkable period of amateur

investigation provided ample fodder for a readership increasingly interested in the details of everyday life and abuse of power and process. When
we link his efforts to those (often higher profile) poverty experts highlighted by other welfare historians, we can garner a much clearer understanding of how seemingly disparate threads of workhouse criticism, which
might be limited in their capacity to create the momentum for change on
their own, could overlap across the English and Welsh welfare landscape
and create a reform movement which was much more influential than the
sum of its parts.

This is not to say that reforming ideas and sentiments gained traction
easily. By taking his personal crusade for workhouse reform before the
widest possible audience via the press, Rowntree often highlighted the
failings of named officers and guardians, and routinely accused whole
Boards of failing to take his criticisms seriously. Unsurprisingly, his mes-
sage was often badly received by officials and others, and the nature of
their responses to his letters is almost as revealing as the letters themselves
when it comes to understanding the power of public opinion and the
potential for workhouse reform in the period.

"A Long Tissue of Captious, Ill-Tempered, Uncharitable Fault Finding": Responses to Rowntree's Criticisms[74]

As an amateur workhouse inspector who chose to use the public medium
of the press to air his views, Joseph Rowntree (like other social investigators) inevitably attracted criticism from those whose judgement and conduct he questioned. One early responder, who signed himself only "A
Guardian from Preston", described Rowntree as "one of those busy meddling persons whose excess of zeal generally leads them into numerous
errors", and contrasted the "misleading" statements of a "stranger, who
only pays a flying visit", to his own, far more positive observations, which,
he wrote, were the result of "visits which I have paid to these establishments during a period of nearly twenty years".[75] His comment once again
reminds us that Rowntree's investigative activity was, by-and-large, quietly
undertaken and without fanfare: it is obvious that the anonymous guardian had never heard of Rowntree, and was unaware that he had been visiting workhouses himself across Britain and Ireland for more than twenty
years. The patronising tone of the guardian's comments epitomise the

kind of responses Rowntree attracted, especially in the early years of his activities, before the sheer number of his published letters made a degree of notoriety unavoidable.[76] In the same year, for example, one of the Leeds guardians remarked "that it was nonsense for the Board to spend their time in replying to these letters, and that they ought to treat them with silent contempt", and the Chairman agreed, adding that it was "below the dignity of the Board" to respond to them.[77] The Master of Alston workhouse was even more dismissive, stating that:

> It is not my intention to open out and explain to your officious correspondent the definite points of law … but as he does not seem very clear on the subject, I would advise him to consult his "Bradshaw," and make the best of his way back to Leeds … leaving the Workhouses in the north to the supervision of men of competency and authority.[78]

This comment on "Bradshaw"—the railway timetable—suggests the Master felt that Rowntree was merely dropping into places that were accessible on the railway from Leeds, and is consistent with a wider set of criticisms of social investigators, social workers and philanthropists operating at this time. We cannot ultimately know how and why Rowntree organised his itinerary, varying as it did across a spectrum between "obvious" large urban workhouses and rather less compelling places, but it would seem likely that he had a network of correspondents and/or had picked up on other seams of public criticism of the places he visited. None of his letters, after all, report an institution with a clean bill of health. While this is only the most likely of several readings, the sense that "intelligence", a core part of the generation of a unified body of public opinion, could join up to create targeted interventions and investigations is important to our argument about workhouse reform. And of course, responses from aggrieved local administrators could only add to this picture.

For many of those who felt stung by Rowntree's criticisms, it was enough merely to point out that he was an outsider and to suggest that he was uninformed. Others, however, allowed the heat of their anger to spill over into print, especially when his tenacity and persistence required them to respond. In 1864, one Huddersfield official loftily informed the periodical press reading public that "The Workhouses of this country are now under not only local, but also Government Inspectors, who carefully and regularly inspect them, much more efficiently than can be done by this

self-appointed and self-opinionated inspector", and compared Joseph
Rowntree of Leeds unfavourably with his more illustrious namesake:

> It is painful to think that the name and fame of a really good man, should be
> endangered by the vagaries of one bearing the same appellation; for the late
> Joseph Rowntree was a true philanthropist. The one who now bears his
> name is but a mere imitator; as ignorant of the law he professes to remedy,
> as he is oblivious of facts.[79]

The criticism that Rowntree was "ignorant of the law" is an interesting
one, echoing as it does the comments by the Master of Alston workhouse;
for it is clear throughout his printed correspondence that he had a very
thorough understanding of the statutory requirements placed upon
guardians, and of the rules which were formulated and disseminated by
the Poor Law Board for the guidance of local officials. More than once, he
quoted directly from William Golden Lumley, Assistant Secretary to the
Poor Law Board and the author of some of the most authoritative works
on the operation of the English and Welsh Poor Laws in the 1850s and
1860s.[80] As his treatment of Hannah Kendrew's case made clear, however,
he also had a very firm grasp of the nuances of the law and of the ways that
it could be made to answer the needs of local officials and unions at the
expense of the welfare of paupers. He was aware, in a way that the Alston
Master was not (or would not admit to being), that both the law and the
Poor Law Board's rules left a great deal to the discretion of local officials
in terms of how paupers were actually treated in individual workhouses. It
was for this reason that, by and large, his criticisms and observations, while
rooted in a thorough knowledge and understanding of poor law procedure, aimed more at the humanitarian failings he found in workhouses
than the illegality of individual officers.

The heated and (at times) intemperate response of many Boards of
Guardians who felt that their entire administrative undertaking with
regard to the union workhouse was being called into question, reflect this
observation.[81] Rowntree was variously described in print as "that cowardly
Quaker", a "wandering stranger" who indulged in a "ridiculous exaggera-
tion of the facts", a "monomaniac" and an "unofficial spy".[82] He was, in a
signal of attempts to shape local public opinion, "Pecksniffian", "ignorant
and illiterate", and a "petty-fogging intermedler and mischief maker".[83] In
an unsigned response covering a whole column of the local news page in
the *Carmarthen Reporter*, one writer took Rowntree's detailed critique to

task point-by-point, adopting the usual condescending tone and calling into question at every stage Rowntree's qualifications to make such criticisms. He ended his caustic reply by stating that:

> It is all very fine for Joseph Rowntree to play the philanthropist, but he must do it in a small way at home, for he is totally unqualified to come the John Howard over Workhouses, and the sooner he leaves off the attempt the better for himself and all parties concerned.[84]

The reference to John Howard, the great prison reformer of the late eighteenth century, is telling. On the one hand, it demonstrates that many of his critics believed Rowntree's efforts on behalf of the workhouse poor were not only misguided but the result of an inflated (and unjustified) sense of his own importance. The *North and South Shields Gazette*, for example, reported that he was "a maniac" in regard to workhouse visitation, and that he "liked to be looked up to as a kind of benevolent philanthropist, like Howard".[85] Yet on the other, it was a comparison that was made admiringly on occasion. The *Gloucester Journal*, for example, suggested that "our guardians ought not to object to ... [t]he periodic visitations of benevolent and practical men, who tread in the footsteps of Howard"; and it went on to describe Rowntree as an "intelligent and philanthropic gentleman" whose "descriptions are not over drawn and [whose] objections can best be answered by removing the evils of which he so justly complains".[86] Much earlier, a correspondent to the *Sheffield and Rotherham Independent* had responded to the Guardians' ill-tempered criticisms of Rowntree by observing that:

> the opinions and suggestions of an acute and disinterested man, devoting a good deal of attention to the inspection of workhouses, and able to compare the condition of one house with that of many others, cannot fail to be worthy of consideration.[87]

Even the editors of the *Dundee, Perth and Cupar Advertiser*—which, perhaps, had more reason than most to mistrust the judgement of a self-appointed English inspector of their poor law institutions—were on Rowntree's side when his findings were savaged by the local parochial authorities. "That a gentlemen of independent means", they wrote:

should at his own charge travel round the country, minutely examining prisons, poor-houses, and all other places where people not of the nicest are
congregated, and that he should be at the trouble of praising what was
praiseworthy, censuring what was faulty, and suggesting whatever his experience told him would be an improvement, seems to have astonished some
persons beyond measure.[88]

Like so many of the Victorian "poverty experts" and social investigators,
Rowntree attracted ire and plaudits in the sphere of press and public opinion. Yet, his presence there, and the fact that he himself was directly
responsible for generating and shaping strands of that public opinion,
demonstrates powerfully the presence of a rapidly evolving reform argument at both local and national levels.

The references to Howard also lead us to consider how Rowntree himself visualised his work as an institutional reformer. For one thing, newspaper commentary reminds us that (*pace* the *Dundee Advertiser*) he also
visited many jails and prisons in England and Scotland, though this aspect
of his work took up much less time and far fewer column inches than that
relating to workhouses.[89] For another, it is clear that although he was
determined to remain independent when it came to his activities (perhaps
sensing that this was the best way to maintain his cherished impartiality)
Rowntree does seem to have understood that his work had its place within
a wider movement for workhouse and institutional reform, broadly
defined. For example, in a letter published in the *Sheffield and Rotherham
Independent* in 1861, in which he revisited the issue of ladies' visiting
committees, Rowntree wrote that:

> I am fully aware that many of the governors of the poor houses are adverse
> to the visits of ladies, however wise and judicious they may prove; even an
> Elizabeth Fry and a Florence Nightingale class would have been rejected by
> some boards of guardians of the poor, their chaplains, and governors.

He went on to observe that "Men without Christian sympathy will ever
and anon thwart the efforts of a Howard, a Clarkson, a Wilberforce, an
Elizabeth Fry or a Florence Nightingale".[90] From this, we can infer that,
privately at least, he did indeed situate his own investigations into workhouse conditions within a venerable tradition of institutional investigation
and reform reaching back to Howard and Elizabeth Fry, but also encom-
passing famous names from his own era, in particular, Florence Nightingale.

Indeed, many of Nightingale's own preoccupations with regard to institutional conditions clearly influenced Rowntree's manifesto, most notably the need for effective ventilation and its effect on the health of patients and inmates, the need for paid and well-trained medical and care staff on the wards, and a condemnation of institutions employing untrained pauper nurses.[91]

Elsewhere, and perhaps even more importantly, Rowntree specifically namechecked Louisa Twining and the Workhouse Visiting Society (WVS), founded only a year before the first of Rowntree's recovered letters was published. As we saw in Chap. 1, Twining established the WVS "to promote the moral and spiritual improvement of workhouse inmates", and listed its main objectives as:

> befriending the destitute and orphan children … the instruction and comfort of the afflicted … [and working] For the benefit of the ignorant and depraved, by assisting the officers of the establishment in forming classes for instruction; in the encouragement of useful occupation during the hours of leisure; or in any other work that may seem to the guardians to be useful and beneficial.[92]

The parallels between the aims and objectives of the WVS and Rowntree's own preoccupations are clear. Rowntree's admiration for Twining and the work of the WVS—which, it is important to note, relied almost entirely on voluntary committees of spiritually motivated women who reached out to workhouse paupers—is clear throughout his newspaper correspondence. He mentioned Twining by name several times in his letters, and drew attention to the work she had initiated under the auspices of the WVS and other voluntary organisations in London. In 1862, in a particularly long and detailed letter on the subject of "The Poor and the Poor Laws" to the *Northampton Mercury*, he wrote, among other things, of the importance of boarding pauper children in schools away from the "contaminating" influence of the workhouse, during the course of which he drew attention to the fact that:

> Louisa Twining, who is the honorary secretary of the Ladies' Visiting Committee in London, gave her evidence, last year, before the Parliamentary Committee (which I had an opportunity of hearing), in favour of unions being allowed to support an institution which she and a few ladies have successfully opened in London for the reception of respectable young women, who, on being out of situations, are homeless and frequently destitute.[93]

Clearly, Rowntree, though ostensibly unaffiliated as an amateur work-house visitor, was significantly influenced by other currents in the wider workhouse reform movement. In particular, he seems to have taken notice of those individuals and organisations which were active in London in the late-1850s and early-1860s (an important point to which we return in Chap. 3), and who were advocating for the "moral and spiritual" reform of workhouse paupers through a number of structural changes in work-house procedure and administration. He even went to the trouble and expense of travelling to London to hear Twining's evidence to the Select Committee of Inquiry into the Administration of the Relief of the Poor in 1861, demonstrating not only his admiration for her work and that of the WVS but also his commitment to workhouse reform more generally. The fact that he recognised the power of the Inquiry as a tool to achieve this end also places Rowntree in a wider (national and international) cadre of social investigators of this period.[94]

Rowntree was a remarkable social investigator, and an influential work-house visitor in his own right. He was exceptional in his dedication and persistence, and in the quiet personal and economic sacrifices he made in touring all four corners of the United Kingdom to gather facts and to publicise irregularities and iniquities. His method was one of minute scru-tiny and exposure of the anecdotal to publicise the systemic: he recognised the value of appealing to the public directly through the press, and his commitment to this approach only strengthened as his disillusion with the Poor Law Board's inspectorate grew. He was not alone in these beliefs, either. In a commentary on a "scandal" at Lambeth Workhouse, the cor-respondent for the *London Daily News* suggested that:

> If it be remembered that the official inspector conducting an inquiry into workhouse abuses combines the functions of judge and jury; that he exam-ines witnesses; sums up evidence and passes the verdict, afterwards put for-ward in the name of the Poor-law Board; it will be seen that complete publicity is one main safeguard for the manner and spirit in which these investigations are conducted.[95]

There were others, too, who followed a similar path to Joseph Rowntree of Leeds in gathering the facts of workhouse deficiencies and the mistreat-ment of paupers, of pressing the poor law authorities in London to take action, and of publicising their concerns in the popular press, and it is to this key group of putative reformers that we turn in the final chapter: that is, workhouse inmates themselves.

NOTES

1. For context see O. Frankel, *States of Inquiry: Social Investigation and Print Culture in Nineteenth-Century Britain and the United States* (Baltimore, 2006), 1–71, and K. Callanan Martin, *Hard and Unreal Advice: Mothers, Social Science and the Victorian Poverty Experts* (Basingstoke, 2008).
2. The original trusts were the Joseph Rowntree Charitable Trust, the Joseph Rowntree Social Service Trust Ltd., and the Joseph Rowntree Village Trust. The modern incarnations of these trusts are the Charitable Trust, the Joseph Rowntree Foundation, the Joseph Rowntree Housing Trust, and the Joseph Rowntree Reform Trust Ltd.
3. Transcription of the 'Founder's Memorandum': https://www.jrf.org.uk/about-us/our-heritage/lasting-vision-change (accessed 16/07/2019).
4. I. Packer, 'Religion and the New Liberalism: the Rowntree family, Quakerism, and social reform', *Journal of British Studies*, 42 (2003), 236–257; M. Freeman, 'Victorian Philanthropy and the Rowntree's: The Joseph Rowntree Charitable Trust', *Quaker Studies*, 7 (2003), 193–213; and A. Vernon, *A Quaker Businessman: The Life of Joseph Rowntree, 1836–1925* (London, 1958).
5. It is certain that many more letters were published in the local press either by, or relating to, Rowntree. In the course of gathering the evidence for this chapter, we came across many references to further newspaper correspondence which it has not been possible to locate. This is of less importance for the present discussion as it might appear: as we demonstrate below, Rowntree's modus operandi followed a similar pattern in all of the towns he visited, so it is unlikely that we have missed anything of importance in terms of his conclusions and suggestions. Nonetheless, it is still a tantalising possibility that even the ca.150 letters analysed here are merely the tip of the iceberg.
6. A common experience for amateur investigators: See G. Ginn, *Culture, Philanthropy and the Poor in Late Victorian London* (London, 2017).
7. On this broader investigatory canvas see C. Hilliard, 'Popular reading and social investigation in Britain, 1850s–1940s', *Historical Journal*, 57 (2014), 247–271; L. Seaber, *Incognito Social Investigation in British Literature: Certainties in Degradation* (Cham, 2017); and O. Frankel, 'Scenes of commission: Royal commissions of inquiry and the culture of social investigation in early Victorian Britain', *The European Legacy*, 4 (1999), 20–41.
8. *Liverpool Mercury*, 28 November 1859 (original emphasis).
9. Ibid.

10. Oxford Dictionary of National Biography (ODNB), entry for James Cropper (1823–1900): https://www-oxforddnb-com.ezproxy4.lib.le. ac.uk/view/10.1093/ref:odnb/9780198614128.001.0001/ odnb-9780198614128-e-38939?rskey=k26Ubq&result=1 (accessed 17/ 07/2019); J. Wake, *Klienwort Benson: The History of Two Families in Banking* (Oxford, 1997), 50.

11. ODNB, entry for James Cropper (1797–1840), https://www-oxforddnb-com.ezproxy4.lib.le.ac.uk/view/10.1093/ref:odnb/97801986 14128.001.0001/odnb-9780198614128-e-6781#odnb-978019861412 8-e-6781 (accessed 17/07/2019).

12. *Liverpool Mercury*, 28 November 1859. Rowntree was also tapping into a rich seam of social investigation and intervention in Liverpool. See A. Wilcox, *The Church and the Slums: The Victorian Anglican Church and its Mission to Liverpool's Poor* (Newcastle, 2014).

13. T. Deane, 'The Professionalisation of Philanthropy: the case of Louisa Twining, 1820–1912' (Unpublished PhD thesis, University of Sussex, 2005), 40.

14. *Newcastle Daily Mail*, 18 January 1862.

15. *Liverpool Mercury*, 28 November 1859. Rowntree was picking up a much deeper and longer-term thread of concern with the nature and utility of work regimes in workhouses. See P. Carter and D. Wileman, 'Managing useless work: The Southwell and Mansfield hand crank of the 1840s', in P. Carter and K. Thompson (eds.), *Pauper Prisons, Pauper Palaces: The Victorian Poor Law in the East and West Midlands 1834–1871* (Kibworth Beauchamp, 2018), 37–56. Resistance to work was also to become a core part of the narrative for the existence of "honest poverty" in the later nineteenth century. See M. Levine Clark, *Unemployment, Welfare and Masculine Citizenship: So Much Honest Poverty in Britain 1870–1930* (Basingstoke, 2015), 28–46.

16. Ibid.

17. *Liverpool Mercury*, 3 December 1859. Rowntree again referred to his time reporting on the Dublin workhouse during the Irish Famine in the *Newcastle Daily Mail*, 18 January 1862, and the *Bradford Observer*, 14 May 1868. It has been impossible so far to verify Rowntree's claims to have done so on behalf of the Irish Poor Law Board, but on the wider culture of outsiders visiting Irish workhouses see S. A. King, *Women, Welfare and Local Politics 1880–1920: "We Might be Trusted"* (Brighton, 2005), 251–257 and V. Crossman, 'Welfare and Nationality: The Poor Laws in Nineteenth-Century Ireland', in J. Stewart and S. A. King (eds.), *Welfare Peripheries: The Development of Welfare States in Nineteenth and Twentieth Century Europe* (Bern, 2007), 67–96.

18. *Bury Times*, 28 January 1860. This observation was distinctly Liberal rather than radical. On this dichotomy see R. Breton, 'Portraits of the poor in early nineteenth century radical journalism', *Journal of Victorian Culture*, 21 (2016), 176. Many of these individual concerns were to become considerable points of contestation in the later nineteenth-century press, giving us a clear sense of Rowntree as an amateur pioneer.
19. Ibid. The language and fact of inspection keyed into a nascent sense, emerging out of the public health movement, that inspection (professional *and* amateur) was the key driver of reform. See C. Hamlin, 'Nuisances and community in mid-Victorian England: the attractions of inspection', *Social History*, 38 (2013), 346–379.
20. Ibid.
21. See E. Midwinter, *Social Administration in Lancashire, 1830–60: Poor Law, Public Health and Police* (Manchester, 1969), and E. Midwinter, 'State intervention at the local level: the new Poor Law in Lancashire', *Historical Journal*, 10 (1967), 106–112. Also A. Gritt and P. Park, 'The workhouse populations of Lancashire in 1881', *Local Population Studies*, 86 (2011), 37–65.
22. *Preston Chronicle*, 28 January 1860. Like Lancashire as a whole, Preston was an obvious choice for an amateur inspector wanting to find fault given the long history of problems in poor law administration there. See W. Proctor, 'Poor law administration in Preston Union, 1838–48', *Transactions of the Historic Society of Lancashire and Cheshire*, 117 (1965), 145–166; L. Darwen, 'Workhouse Populations of the Preston Union, 1841–61', *Local Population Studies*, 93 (2014), 33–53; L. Darwen, 'Implementing and administering the New Poor Law in the industrial north: A case study of Preston union in regional context, 1837–1861' (Unpublished PhD thesis, Nottingham Trent University, 2015).
23. This theme of duties of care is taken up in Chap. 3.
24. *Preston Chronicle*, 28 January 1860.
25. This "manifesto" has considerable resonance with some of the concerns of medical journals, clerics, philanthropists interested in child welfare and public health specialists in the later nineteenth century. See Martin, *Hard and Unreal Advice*.
26. The term "vagrant" has deep roots in English linguistic and social history. During the nineteenth-century it came to be first augmented and then replaced by the term casual. The latter was essentially an administrative term written into the New Poor Law and inscribed into the fabric of workhouses in the sense that they were supposed to have "casual wards" to provide short-term accommodation for vagrants. This linguistic and categorical change is symbolically important, signalling a shift in conceptions

of vagrancy from a moral, socio-cultural or economic issue to an administrative one.

27. The issue of vagrancy has, as A. Eccles, *Vagrancy in Law and Practice under the Old Poor Law* (Abingdon, 2012) notes, received considerably more attention under the Old Poor law than the new. On post-1834 see D. J. V. Jones, '"A Dead Loss to the Community": the Criminal Vagrant in Mid-Nineteenth Century Wales', *Welsh History Review*, 8 (1976), 312–344; A. Tanner, 'The Casual Poor and the City of London Poor Law Union, 1837–1869', *Historical Journal*, 42 (1999), 183–206; R. Vorspan, 'Vagrancy and the New Poor Law in Late-Victorian and Edwardian England', *English Historical Review*, 92 (1977), 59–81. For a totemic article on early modern vagrancy see: P. Slack, 'Vagrants and Vagrancy in England, 1598–1664', *Economic History Review*, 27 (1974), 360–379.

28. L. Rose, *Rogues and Vagabonds: Vagrant Underworld in Britain 1815–1985* (London, 1985).

29. The elision of poverty, dependence and contagion was not unique to the vagrant in this period, but it was a particularly strong one. See A. Hansen, 'Exhibiting Vagrancy, 1851: Victorian London and the 'Vagabond Savage"', *Literary London: Interdisciplinary Studies in the Representation of London*, 2 (2004), available online at http://www.literarylondon.org/london-journal/september2004/hansen.html (accessed 11/11/2019); S. Koven, *Slumming: Sexual and Social Politics in Victorian London* (Princeton, 2004), 31–70; and B. Althammer, 'Controlling Vagrancy: Germany, England and France, 1880–1914', in B. Althammer, L. Raphael and T. Stazic-Wendt (eds.), *Rescuing the Vulnerable: Poverty, Welfare and Social Ties in Modern Europe* (Oxford, 2016), 187–211.

30. *Justice of the Peace, and County, Borough, Poor Law Union, and Parish Law Recorder*, Vol. 12, No. 18, 29 April, 1848, 274.

31. M. A. Crowther, *The Workhouse System, 1834–1929: The History of an English Social Institution* (London, 1981), 249.

32. Crowther, *Workhouse System*, 250–251; D. Englander, *Poverty and Poor Law Reform in 19th Century England: From Chadwick to Booth* (Abingdon, 1998), 32–33.

33. Crowther, *Workhouse System*, 251. Also A. L. Beier, '"Takin' it to the streets": Henry Mayhew and the language of the underclass in mid-nineteenth-century London', in A. L. Beier and P. Ocobock (eds.), *Cast Out: Vagrancy and Homelessness in Global and Historical Perspective* (Athens, OH, 2008), 88–116.

34. Crowther, *Workhouse System*. Also F. Driver, *Power and Pauperism: The Workhouse System, 1834–1884* (Cambridge, 1993), 89.

35. Englander, *Poverty and Poor Law Reform*, 33. B. Althammer, 'Roaming Men, Sedentary Women? The Gendering of Vagrancy Offenses in

Nineteenth-Century Europe', *Journal of Social History*, 51 (2018), 736–759.

36. The focus on Northampton is not, of course, accidental. Like all significant midland urban areas sitting on major transport routes, vagrancy had been a perennial and large sale problem which only worsened in the nineteenth-century. Rowntree clearly selected this town deliberately.
37. *Northampton Mercury*, 24 May 1862.
38. Ibid. (original emphasis).
39. *Nottingham Daily Express*, 5 March 1865 (original emphasis). This narrative is also one we see emerging in London at a later date. See M. Brodie, 'Artisans and dossers: the 1886 West End riots and the East End casual poor', *London Journal*, 24 (1999), 34–50.
40. M. Freeman, '"Journeys into poverty kingdom": complete participation and the British vagrant, 1866–1914', *History Workshop Journal*, 52 (2001), 99–121.
41. *Liverpool Mercury*, 21 May 1866.
42. Ibid.
43. Seaber, *Incognito Social Investigation*; D. Taylor, 'Beyond the bounds of respectable society: The "dangerous classes" in Victorian and Edwardian England', in J. Rowbotham and K. Stevenson (eds.), *Criminal Conversations: Victorian Crimes, Social Panic and Moral Outrage* (Columbus OH., 2005), 3–22.
44. *Leeds Mercury*, 2 March 1863.
45. The rules regarding who could and could not be relieved in a particular place under the English and Welsh poor laws are complex, but in essence a person could only be relieved where they had a legal settlement. In the first instance, a person's place of settlement was likely to be the same as their father's or the place where they were born, but as an adult one could gain a settlement elsewhere by a number of different means. For the definitive treatment of settlement law see K. D. M. Snell, *Parish and Belonging: Community, Identity and Welfare in England and Wales 1700–1950* (Cambridge, 2006).
46. We encounter this genre of story consistently in the letters and enquiries that underpin our wider AHRC project 'In Their Own Write'.
47. *Leeds Mercury*, 2 March 1863. This was not strictly true. See Snell, *Parish and Belonging*, 58–63.
48. Ibid.
49. Martin, *Hard and Unreal Advice*.
50. Crumpsall workhouse was opened in 1857 as a supplement to, rather than a replacement for, the old workhouse in Bridge Street.

51. In this process of simply hanging around near the workhouse Rowntree follows other literary and investigative figures of the period. See L. Foster, 'The representation of the Workhouse in Nineteenth-Century Culture' (Unpublished PhD thesis, University of Cardiff, 2014).

52. *Manchester Courier*, 6 March 1866.

53. Ibid.

54. Other social investigators in the later nineteenth-century were less prone to advocacy but nonetheless used similar methods and high profile and anecdotal cases to further their research and enhance its public bite. See contributions to J. Bradhsaw and R. Sainsbury (eds.), *Getting the Measure of Poverty: The Early Legacy of Seebohm Rowntree* (Aldershot, 2000), and A. Gillie, 'Identifying the poor in the 1870s and 1880s', *Economic History Review*, 61 (2008), 302–325.

55. Ibid.

56. The National Archives (hereafter, TNA), MH 12/6058, Joseph Rowntree to the Poor Law Board (hereafter PLB), 7 March 1866. For more on the MH12 archive see P. Carter and N. Whistance, *Living the Poor Life: A Guide to the Poor Law Union Correspondence, c.1834 to 1871* (London, 2011).

57. Rowntree engaged directly with the PLB on a number of occasions in relation to the conditions at specific workhouses, most notably those at Bradford and, intriguingly (given the possible family connection), York (see TNA MH 12/14736 and 14408). But it was in relation to Manchester that this kind of approach found its clearest—and most extensive—expression.

58. TNA MH 12/6058, Joseph Rowntree to the PLB, 7 March 1866.

59. TNA MH 12/6058, Joseph Rowntree to the PLB, 14 April 1868.

60. In these assertions, Rowntree was echoing a wider narrative about the failings of medical care in New Poor Law institutions. For a summary see S. A. King, 'Poverty, medicine and the workhouse in the eighteenth and nineteenth centuries', in J. Reinarz and L. Schwarz (eds.), *Medicine and the Workhouse* (Rochester, 2013), 228–251.

61. TNA MH 12/6058, Joseph Rowntree to the PLB, 16 April 1866. On the politics of workhouse food and the workhouse diet, see N. Durbach, *Many Mouths: The Politics of Food in Britain from the Workhouse to the Welfare State* (Cambridge, 2020), Chapter 1: 'Old English Fare: Festive Meals, the New Poor Law, and the Boundaries of Nation'.

62. TNA MH 12/6058, Joseph Rowntree to the PLB, 5 May 1866.

63. Ibid. This elision of prison and workhouse is one that paupers themselves used (as we see in Chap. 3) and which underpinned some of the dissenting voices on deterrence reviewed in Chap. 1.

64. TNA MH 12/6058, Joseph Rowntree to the PLB, 5 May 1866.

65. TNA MH 12/6058, Joseph Rowntree to the PLB, 9 May 1866.

66. *Newcastle Daily Mail,* 17 January 1862.
67. *Carlisle Journal,* 4 March 1862. The language here decidedly reflects that which underpins the notion of a tribunal of the public. See C. Brant, '"The tribunal of the public": Eighteenth century letters and the politics of vindication', in C. Bland and M. Cross (eds.), *Gender and Politics in the Age of Letter Writing, 1750–2000* (Aldershot, 2004), 15–28.
68. TNA MH 12/6058, Joseph Rowntree to the PLB, 31 March 1866 and 12 April 1866.
69. TNA MH 12/6058, Joseph Rowntree to the PLB, 14 April 1866.
70. Ibid.
71. *Leeds Mercury,* 4 July 1860.
72. *Rochdale Observer,* 10 March 1860.
73. P. Gurney, *Wanting and Having: Popular Politics and Liberal Consumerism in England 1830–1870* (Manchester, 2015), *passim*; S. Shave, '"Immediate Death or a Life of Torture Are the Consequences of the System": the Bridgwater Union Scandal and Policy Change', in Reinarz and Schwarz, *Medicine and the Workhouse,* 164–191.
74. The quotation is from the *Cardiff Times,* 23 December 1864.
75. *Preston Chronicle,* 4 February 1860. To be an elected guardian for this length of time was not unknown, but this comment may suggest a pattern of visiting in several capacities.
76. Many early workhouse visiting committees, because they were specifically formed to hold guardians and staff to account by amateurs, attracted similar criticisms. Such attitudes persisted even into the 1880s and early 1890s. See King, *Women, Work, Passim.*
77. *Leeds Mercury,* 5 April 1860.
78. *Carlisle Journal,* 3 July 1862.
79. *Huddersfield Chronicle,* 1 February 1864.
80. *Manchester Courie*r, 7 March 1866; *Bradford Observer,* 15 March 1866. Lumley's published works included *The Law of Parochial Assessments Explained* (2nd ed., London 1853); *The Poor Removal and Union Chargeability Acts* (London, 1865); and several *Manuals of the Duties of Poor Law Officers,* including *The Master and Matron of the Workhouse* (2nd. ed., London, 1869).
81. This sort of outrage may also, of course, have masked a sense that Rowntree was compromising the civic pride of these places, some of which was vested in quality public administration and the buildings that went with it, including workhouses. For a review of the complexities of local belief systems in this regard, see S. Morgan, 'John Deakin Heaton and the "elusive civic pride of the Victorian middle class"', *Urban History,* 45 (2018), 595–615.
82. *Rochdale Observer,* 10 March 1860; *Dundee, Perth and Cupar Advertiser,* 22 March 1861; *Newcastle Daily Mail,* 19 January 1865.

83. *Cardiff Times*, 23 December 1864; *Carmarthen Reporter*, 24 December 1864; *Huddersfield Chronicle*, 2 January 1864.
84. *Carmarthen Reporter*, 17 September 1864.
85. *North and South Shields Gazette*, 20 January 1865. Other unfavourable comparisons between Rowntree and John Howard appear in the *Cardiff Times*, 23 December 1864, and *Potter's Electric News*, 11 January 1865. The comparison is also backward-looking, emphasising our conclusions in Chap. 1 about the essential continuity between pre- and post-1834 attitudes towards workhouses and the poor.
86. *Gloucester Journal*, 27 April 1867. This sort of comment mirrors an increasingly positive press and public commentary on workhouse visiting and those who organised and ran visiting committees.
87. *Sheffield and Rotherham Independent*, 17 March 1860.
88. *Dundee, Perth and Cupar Advertiser*, 22 March 1861.
89. Rowntree claimed to have visited many prisons, but with the exception of the Leeds Borough Gaol in his home town, he tended to restrict his comments to the "prison system" overall. His activities in this area seem to have been concentrated between 1860 and 1864. See, for example, his letters on the subject in the *Leeds Mercury*, 10 September 1860, 17 November 1860, and 8 and 20 August 1864; the *York Gazette*, 19 and 24 April 1862; the *Durham County Advertiser*, 25 April 1862; and the *Northampton Mercury*, 21 June 1862. For context see W. Forsythe, *The State of Prisons in Britain 1775–1900* (London, 8 vols., 2000).
90. *Sheffield and Rotherham Independent*, 10 December 1861.
91. For Context see C. Helmstadter and J. Godden, *Nursing Before Nightingale, 1815–1899* (Farnham, 2011) and contributions to A. Borsay and B. Hunter (eds.), *Nursing and Midwifery in Britain since 1700* (Basingstoke, 2012).
92. Report on the founding of the WVS, *Lloyd's Weekly Newspaper*, 8 August 1858.
93. *Northampton Mercury*, 24 May 1862. For a discussion of wider narratives of contamination, physical and moral, in workhouses, see the review essay by D. Brown, 'Workers, workhouses, and the sick poor: Health and institutional health care in the long nineteenth century', *Journal of Urban History*, 43 (2017), 180–188.
94. See Frankel, *States of Inquiry*.
95. *London Daily News*, 1 November 1866.

CHAPTER 3

Pauper Letter Writers and the Workhouse Experience

Abstract Our third chapter switches attention away from middle-class reformers and investigators to the crucial question of how far the poor had agency to participate in, inform and shape a workhouse reform movement. We show how the poor (residents and former residents of the workhouse) were able to write to the central authorities and to contest the treatment they received and the regimes to which they were subject. Developing this theme, we focus in particular on four extraordinary paupers who wrote multiple letters both on their own behalf and for others in the workhouses where they found themselves. These four men may have had their individual and personal issues with guardians and workhouse staff, but such concerns always developed into much wider manifestos and agendas for workhouse reform which show a remarkable symmetry with sentiments and concrete recommendations in the wider court of public opinion. Over tens of thousands of words to the central authorities, they raised similar points to Joseph Rowntree and, like him, they sought not to overthrow the workhouse system but to make it work as intended. Such men demonstrate remarkable agency and we show how they tried actively to shape, rather than merely reflect or respond to, a wider seam of public opinion from the 1860s that came to support workhouse reform.

© The Author(s) 2020   73
P. Jones, S. King, *Pauper Voices, Public Opinion and Workhouse
Reform in Mid-Victorian England*,
https://doi.org/10.1007/978-3-030-47839-1_3

INTRODUCTION

As Chap. 1 suggested, the workhouse was a subject of great ambivalence for the Victorian public just as it had been for most of the Georgian period. It was simultaneously viewed in public and professional debate as an inevitable (even necessary) part of the welfare landscape, and an unsettlingly harsh receptacle for the incarceration of the deserving poor. Towards the end of the New Poor Law, as calls for the abolition of the mixed workhouse strengthened, this long-standing ambivalence was replaced by an unstoppable tide of hostility that finally broke on the shores of the Liberal Welfare Reforms in the early-twentieth century.[1] At a stroke, in 1913, the workhouse, which had dominated the landscape of institutional welfare for almost two centuries, was gone, to be replaced by "Poor Law institutions". Yet this was a change in name only, and it took a further sixteen years and the passing of a Conservative measure (the Local Government Bill of 1929) before the New Poor Law and its administrative structures were officially abolished, and a further twenty years before the investment needed for the specialised care of most workhouse residents could be found.[2] Arguably, it is in this liminal period between the development of a broad consensus that the mixed workhouse must be done away with and its structural replacement with the institutions of the welfare state that the popular memory we retain of it today settled in the public imagination.

There is no doubt that the horror of the Victorian workhouse is a remarkably enduring trope. Indeed, its influence shows no sign of abating for social historians, authors of popular fiction, or for the mainstream media.[3] Since the "workhouse test" was the central deterrent policy of the New Poor Law, one crafted to provide the meanest safety net so that only the least fortunate and most desperate would submit to it, one can easily understand the common view of workhouse inmates as a downtrodden and despairing mass, "a passive emblem of the misery of the nineteenth century", to quote Anne Crowther.[4] There is, of course, justification for this view. It is undoubtedly true that many paupers resisted entering the workhouse, fighting to retain what little independence they had outside of it.[5] It is also true that the architects of the New Poor Law were at times explicit in their desire to eliminate the last threads of that independence at the workhouse door.[6] Moreover, historians have (as we have already seen in Chaps. 1 and 2) begun in earnest to dissect both high profile and lesser known scandals, revealing significant instances of abuse in workhouses. Even in the many places that avoided scandal, a sojourn in the workhouse as a child or young adult has been viewed as incurring a lifelong penalty in terms of socio-economic prospects.[7] And, of course, the activities of amateur social investigators like Joseph Rowntree revealed many everyday shortcomings in workhouse regimes short of systemic abuse. It is thus unsurprising that many have found it difficult to see past the demoralising and de-personalising effect of the Victorian workhouse.

This is further underpinned by the fact that remarkably little scholarship has emerged on the actual experience of workhouse paupers since the publication of Anne Crowther's ground-breaking study almost 40 years ago. Yet, when we look beyond the conventional sources informing both popular narratives and academic histories, it is possible to find evidence for an alternative view of some aspects of workhouse life. David Green's commanding work on pauper protest in nineteenth-century London, for example, forces us to challenge the latent view in much of the historiography that inmates were completely powerless and entirely lacked agency.[8] In particular, he highlights the problem faced by local officials in trying to subdue paupers who had a clear notion of their "rights" under the New Poor Law—or, more accurately, those who had a good grasp of the legal and moral obligations of union officials towards them and who felt that those obligations had not been fulfilled. Such inmates had a clear idea of the minimum standard of care they could expect to receive, and they were often prepared to fight, sometime doggedly, to ensure that their treatment did not drop below those standards.[9] Green is not alone in suggesting a deeper and more nuanced view of the character, conduct and meaning of workhouse life. Jeff James, for example, has recently undertaken a fusion of local and central records for a single pauper in the Ampthill Union workhouse which shows that young women could exercise very considerable agency vis-à-vis staff who were often powerless to control them.[10] More widely, Steven King argued in both 2017 and 2019 that historians had been unduly pessimistic about the nature of workhouse life and have systematically overstated the capacity of workhouse staff to employ regulation and punishment as tools to effectively control inmates.[11] Such views have been echoed by Peter Higginbotham, who argues that a failure to find and listen to the voices of workhouse inmates has fostered an overwhelmingly negative view of the oppressed workhouse pauper.[12]

A more nuanced appreciation of the ways that paupers experienced and negotiated workhouse life is not, however, beyond our grasp. For example, David Green utilised one source which is of particular interest to this endeavour: the great wealth of letters sent from local unions to the Poor

Law Commission and its successors in London, through the close reading of which he was able to build narratives of protest and insubordination by named paupers.[13] Green's work focussed on the commissioners' correspondence largely from the point of view of letters sent, and replies received, by local poor law officials. But as David Englander reminded us almost 20 years ago, it is also possible to use this archive to gain a more direct sense of how inmates navigated workhouse life.[14] The volumes of correspondence received by the commissioners contain a significant number of letters from paupers themselves, and it is on these that we will focus in the present chapter. Letters came from both indoor and outdoor paupers and they cover the full range of concerns faced by them. Almost invariably, however, indoor paupers raised concerns about ill-treatment, malpractice, inmate relations, diet and punishment in the workhouse: in other words, precisely those issues that were raised by Joseph Rowntree in his letters and correspondence, and which were highlighted by Green in his work on pauper protest in London. Most of the paupers who wrote to the commissioners did so only once or twice, but there are exceptions: some paupers wrote many letters over time. The concerns and complaints they expressed about the treatment of workhouse inmates, and the observations they made about the workhouse experience overall, are consistent with those found in the letters of paupers who wrote sparingly.[15] Yet, the detail contained in these examples of serial correspondence, and the rich narratives that unfold over time, mean that it is uniquely possible to get "under the skin" of these letter writers, to see beyond their immediate concerns and gain some idea of the motivations that lay behind their considerable efforts in writing. As we shall see, it is also possible to place the actions of these pauper correspondents within the wider currents of workhouse criticism emerging from the 1850s onwards which are discussed at length in Chaps. 1 and 2, and to trace how such writers conceived of the importance of public opinion and the power of the press in their efforts to secure remedy both for themselves and paupers more widely.

This sort of epistolary engagement over welfare (and particularly the presence of serial writers) must be regarded as part of a story going back to the Old Poor Law and the 1780s, much as was the case with concerns over workhouses themselves. Prior to 1834, those who fell into need but were outside their parish of settlement either had to return to that parish or write to request that relief be sent to them in a host community.[16] Their letters deployed a rich rhetorical toolbox in order to facilitate claims including highly charged narratives of starvation and nakedness, direct allusions to the laws and regulations that governed their care, and the ubiquitous threat to throw themselves entirely on their parish of settlement if relief at a distance was refused.[17] The poor in the last decades of the Old Poor Law had, therefore, built up a deep tradition of negotiating relief which must have informed their attitudes to the new authorities constituted after 1834, as we suggested in Chap. 1. Indeed, by the 1830s, many of them had also developed a series of strategies to exert pressure on the officials to whom they wrote, including (importantly, for the themes discussed here) the garnering of local publicity for their cases in newspapers and other outlets as "tribunals of the public".[18] Yet, whereas the letters written under the Old Poor Law have gained increasing attention, those of the post-1834 period have lain unused in the tortuous MH12 archive. In this chapter, we investigate the complex epistolary lives of four serial letter writers, three of whom were inmates in East London workhouses—Poplar and Bethnal Green—between 1862 and 1885, and the fourth being resident in the workhouse at Pwllheli, North Wales, in 1868. These dates are partly driven by the availability of sources, but there is also a wider logic in the sense that they encompass what might be conceptualised as the "middle period" of the New Poor Law, the years in which it became apparent that the aims of those who framed the 1834 act were not being met and when the crusade against outdoor relief outlined in Chap. 1 gained traction.[19] While both of the London unions have a significant footprint in the existing poor law historiography, Pwllheli does not, and its inclusion here acts as a counterweight to the assumption (discussed at length in Chap. 1) that these issues were solely experienced in the capital.[20] Overall, this discussion of the experience and agency of workhouse paupers in their own right adds a new and important dimension to our understanding of popular sentiment towards the New Poor Law across England and Wales, suggesting in part why social investigators like Rowntree found such a ready audience.

The four individuals who underpin our analysis wrote a total of 32 letters of complaint consisting of just over 40,000 words. They displayed remarkable eloquence and levels of literacy.[21] They are men (and exclusively men) who went to some lengths to emphasise their "respectability", and it becomes clear that some of them had enjoyed positions of status in their previous lives. In at least one case, we can read the thoughts and opinions of an inmate who had himself once been a parish officer. Nonetheless, it is important to note that the concerns about which they wrote were precisely those that were raised by most inmates, as well as by others, such as Joseph Rowntree, who advocated on behalf of the indoor poor. Indeed, despite the deep seam of grievance that unfolds in these letters there is no sense that their authors viewed themselves as qualitatively different to any other "respectable" inmates in the workhouse.[22] One of the main themes running through these and other similar letters is that although the writers began by lamenting deficiencies in their own treatment, they generally used this as a springboard for a much broader set of complaints about the conditions in the house, and about the behaviour of union officials and the shortcomings of local workhouse administrators. What is notable about the correspondents presented here is that in each case, over many thousands of words, their complaints built into a campaign to see the injustices they witnessed addressed by the authorities. In this sense, they were not so different to Joseph Rowntree. Moreover, each of them acknowledged that there was a personal cost for waging such a campaign, in terms of harsh treatment and retributive punishment by the officers they accused, much as Rowntree himself experienced visceral responses to his letters. Yet each pauper persisted over many months and, sometimes, years. In the final section, it is argued that their careers as inmates coincided with the period of growing public interest in, and concern over, the real experiences of workhouse paupers which are discussed at some length in Chaps. 1 and 2, and that, as highly literate and morally conscientious individuals, they considered it their duty to bring the shortcomings of local officials to the attention of the commissioners. But it is also clear from the nature and extent of their correspondence, and sometimes explicitly from its content, that each of these writers recognised the value of appealing to public opinion beyond the local and central poor law. In this, we argue that they were encouraged, not only by the growing public interest in published accounts, but also by other mid- to late-Victorian trends, including the growth of social investigation (*pace* Rowntree), first-person journalistic exposés, and an expanding interest in autobiographical literature, especially that of subaltern citizens.[23]

More than this, however, the existence of these letters (and the nature of the administrative responses to them) reveals much about the ways that pauper inmates navigated workhouse life and, hence, they are of significant historiographical interest in and of themselves. Despite the fact that workhouse complaints under the New Poor Law emerged at a time when public petitioning had reached unprecedented levels, there is very little of the spirit of supplication or formality in them. In general, they are direct, determined and bold in their demands. They demonstrate that workhouse paupers were far from cowed or submissive, no matter how harsh the regimes they were subjected to. Indeed, the assertiveness of these writers in the face of considerable structural disadvantages is remarkable. Yet, it is again important to note once again that, aside from their literary accomplishment, the letters themselves are unexceptional: these writers are only distinctive because of the scale of the traces they left behind. Moreover, like many other public critics of welfare, all of them sought to change the system as it was, not to propose radical alternatives. There was thus a seamless connection between the strands of "public" opinion on the need for and potential nature of workhouse reform in this period. To explore the broad issues of agency, experience, workhouse relations, the tribunal of the public and the literacy and literary abilities of the poor, we consider the letters and stories of each of our four paupers in turn.

THOMAS GOULD, POPLAR WORKHOUSE

As far as we know, Thomas Gould wrote the first of his letters to the Poor Law Board in August 1853. He began boldly, framing his complaint with little preamble:

> I most Respectfully and Humbly take the liberty to address your Honourable Board with an obedient hope that in so doing I draw your Lordships attention to the very many cases of oppression practised upon the Inmates of the Poplar Union Workhouse, by the Master of that Establishment, and trust that the facts Here Stated and which can be proved, will call fourth your Lordship's attention, and investigation. Your Honourable Board [...] could [n]ever have contemplated—nor Intended that unnecessary Harshness and tyranny should be exercised over *quiet orderly* aged and *afflicted* poor.[24]

Gould then went on to list in meticulous detail the complaints of the elderly poor in the workhouse, including long hours of labour, the onerous nature of the work regime, and the inadequate food (there being "No Indulgence by the Common diate [*diet*] of the House"). These complaints are familiar enough from the historiography, much of the literary representation of workhouse life, and from the letters of Joseph Rowntree. Yet, having laid out his grievances, Gould then asked, rhetorically: "Surely My Lords this Cannot be right[,] this which ought to be an asylum for the aged and afflicted to be made worse than the Criminal's sel [*cell*]".[25] Only then did Gould hint that he had himself been a victim of harsh treatment by the workhouse master, for:

> within [a] few minutes of the time prescribed for quiting Labour and whilst Reading a morral tract, I was [...] told by the Master I should not Read—and thereupon [he] ordered my Books to be taken from me—threatening at the same time to lock me up [and] Calling me an Insolent [*sic*].[26]

In fact, Gould only included this personal example in order to illustrate the wider point about the poor treatment of the aged and impotent poor in the Poplar workhouse. He proceeded to explain that he had been an inmate in the workhouse for "upwards of two years, and have on more than one or two occasions Received from the Master Harsh Ill temper and Tyrannical treatment for which I have not given cause". Nonetheless, Gould maintained that he had "oft times been the Means of preventing Insubordination amongst others by preservative means"—an aspect of workhouse life that historians have mostly failed to observe. Gould was, by his own account, a model inmate, and the sobriety and decorum of his own conduct was clearly intended to contrast directly with that of the workhouse master.[27] But should this prove inadequate to persuade the commissioners of the justice of his cause, he informed them that he "had the Honour to fill several parochial positions over period of about 30 years", and that he had "Favourable testimonials Recorded on the Books of the respective parishes where I have served".[28]

Gould anticipated that the commissioners might "ask if I have ever made [complaint] to the Board of Guardians at their weekly meeting":

> I answer no, and the Reason is this, The Master Has held his situation as Master and His wife as Mattron about 23 years[,] has brought up a large Family, part of whom are still Residing at the Union[,] and the principals of the Guardians are the same from the time of the Union of Poplar, Bromley, and Bow, and I think too Connected for any redriss of Grivance.[29]

This sense that guardians would always back their long-serving staff is something that was also noted when unions and the central authorities were obliged to investigate medical scandals.[30] Nonetheless, Gould trusted that "your Honourable Board will not object to Investigate into Matters", a call for central inquisition that exactly mirrors those made by Rowntree in his own correspondence with the central authorities.

Yet it is already clear, even in his first letter, that Gould's ambitions were more wide-ranging than merely to complain about the treatment of the elderly and afflicted poor. He stated that "there is a want of Sistem in all respects", so that "all are huddled together, the young and the Old the Blind the lame and diseased"; that there was a lack of "proper order"; and that "swearing, blasphemy, Obsenity, of a disgusting nature, and the worst of Filthy Habits [are] practiced".[31] These accusations mirror those levelled at London workhouses in particular by campaigning tracts and fictional texts at all stages of the New Poor Law, an observation that will become important later in this chapter.[32] More than this, in accusing not only the master and matron, but the "want of sistem" in the running of the workhouse, he appeared to be implicating the entire regime including the Board of Guardians, much as other critics of the deterrent workhouse had done for some time. This letter was the first of many that Gould sent to the commissioners, and it was by no means his longest—even at six sides of closely written script—or his most strident. His correspondence did, at least, result in a local investigation into the allegations—a significant outcome in itself, and a wider symbol of the potential for pauper agency for other inmates. But his next letter made it clear that Gould believed this inquiry to have been little more than a smokescreen, much as Joseph Rowntree came to have no faith in the inspection system: "[H]ad your Lordships Assistant Commissioner Called [me] before the Board the whole would have been proved", he wrote, "But your Lordships Assistant thought there was no necessity to do so [and] after an Investigation of 3 hours & 40 minutes I was told to withdraw".[33] Even so, Gould remained steadfast, expanding on his allegations in his next letter, which was written a full two years after the last. In this letter, Gould conceded that, following the investigation into the master's conduct, "for some little time […] there was Considerable improvement" in the workhouse. He also noted that the master was fined £100 and suspended for three months—no small achievement, given that he, as an inmate, seems to have been instrumental in bringing it about. However, he went on to state that "it was but for short duration, when it again relapsed into its former state […] and continues to be so without the appearance of improvement".[34]

Gould also lamented again that he had "been perpetually annoyed and insulted by the Master and Matron[,] by the Guardians, and I may say by many of the Inmates", implying that this harassment was the result of his having challenged the regime in the first place, and testimony to an undercurrent of low-level enduring hostilities within the workhouse which we rarely see in the historiography. Nonetheless, he devoted the remaining three-quarters of this third letter—more than 2500 words—to a further detailed denunciation of the deficiencies and cruelties at Poplar workhouse. These ranged from medical negligence and (once again) the poor diet, to the treatment of vagrants and the cruelty visited on inmates by the matron. He accused the master of negligence, and of being distracted by a timber business which he had set up with his son, something expressly forbidden according to the Poor Law Board's own rules.[35] Gould gave specific instances of paupers who, he believed, had died for want of medical attention.[36] Finally, he stated that the workhouse was so negligently run that "at least one Third of the Inmates are not parishioners"—that is, they did not have a legal right to claim relief in Poplar—"which is a cost to the parish of at least £1500 a year".[37]

In reading Gould's letters, one is struck by the forensic detail he laid down in them, a level of detail entirely reminiscent of the way that social investigators of this period used anecdote to explore the scale, experience and causes of poverty as we saw in Chaps. 1 and 2. All of the main themes were visited again and again. At times, he simply repeated his allegations, but often he elaborated on a theme, and presented further examples to support the case.[38] Indeed, Gould revisited his allegations so many times in the six years of his correspondence, during the whole of which he remained an inmate in the workhouse, and it is unsurprising that he laid himself open to persecution. Nonetheless, the thing that marks out his approach, other than the longevity of his correspondence and the sheer quantity of evidence he submitted, is that he clearly believed himself to be well situated and, indeed, fully entitled to offer his opinions on the systemic failures in Poplar. As we have seen, he described himself as a model inmate, conducting himself "with propriety" and assisting in the preservation of peace in the workhouse when necessary. He also suggested, rather ambitiously, that he was "incapable of falsehood [or] Any thing that is base or low", and that "I never tell an untruth".[39] More than once, Gould offered testimonials to prove his claims about himself. In his third letter, he once again noted that he had had "long Intercourse with parochial officers over a period of 35 years (and that too without a blemish on my character, nor in Moral rectitude)".[40] In his fifth letter, he elaborated on this theme, writing that:

> in the years [18]16, 17, 18 and 19, I was engaged in attempting a sistem of employment, in most of the workhouses within the bill of Mortality and

Succeeded in Establishing a Manufactory for the Employment of the able adult and Infant Poor in many of the Workhouses in and about London and have had the Honour to hold this office for a period of 35 years as Superintendent of Labour, and as master of [a] Workhouse.[41]

It has not been possible to corroborate Gould's claims to long and active parochial service, but they would go some way towards explaining why he felt able not only to bring the charges he did against the Poplar union officials, which he believed were endemic to unions across London, but also to suggest a comprehensive set of reforms that he felt was necessary to put right those injustices. These included: placing the oversight of unions into the hands of government; appointing paid guardians, and disqualifying local ratepayers from holding such office; restricting guardians' continuous service to a maximum of three years; and restricting masters to ten years continuous service in a single workhouse.[42] Such an agenda speaks powerfully to Gould's own knowledge of best practice under the New Poor Law (remarkable in itself) and to a wider seam of discontent at this time among public commentators that (as we saw in Chaps. 1 and 2) the essential purpose and sentiment of the New Poor Law was being subverted by poor local administration and the weakness of central oversight. The poor law was not *meant* to operate in ways he described, and Gould knew it.

As we follow the progress of his long correspondence with the Poor Law Board, it becomes clear that Thomas Gould was motivated by considerably more than a basic sense of personal grievance, or even outrage at the treatment he observed being meted out to others. There was something crusading in his relentless pursuit of those he believed to have failed in their duty and in his defence of the workhouse cohort overall. At one point, he wrote that "In stead […] of calling it an asylum for the aged and Infirm, it ought to be written up in large characters, Tyranny [and] Inhumanity", and he frequently used variants of a rhetoric that he was motivated only by "a duty Which I owe to my Country[,] to its Laws, To your Honourable Board, to the aged & Infirm, And lastly to myself".[43] The conceptual link between Gould and Rowntree, both of whom employed these essential sentiments, is clear. By invoking the language of moral duty, as well as the classic tropes of nineteenth-century Liberalism, Gould elevated his campaign beyond mere complaint, and situated himself as more than just a downtrodden pauper. He was the epitome of a poor writer with agency and a clear understanding of how to navigate and

contest the workhouse regime, two of the key thematic gaps in the literature with which we started this chapter. Moreover, it is unthinkable that
his crusade did not gain notoriety, and probably support, among the other
inmates of the Poplar workhouse, providing some sense of how agency
and a belief in the right to be heard could be transmitted across the pauper
cohort. This is an important observation once we also note that Gould's
persistence and the extent of his reforming evangelism were unusual
among workhouse letter writers, but they were by no means unique.

MUNGO PAUMIER, BETHNAL GREEN WORKHOUSE

Mungo Paumier first entered the Bethnal Green workhouse in 1862,
arriving at a volatile time in its history. By the late-1850s, a steady trickle
of complaints against workhouse officials had become a torrent. The result
was that by the mid-1860s, there was a whole regime change, with the
dismissal of the workhouse master and matron, the resignation of the
schoolmistress, and disciplinary proceedings against two porters, a paid
nurse, and two medical officers.[44] Much of Paumier's first letter protested
at having been forcibly ejected from the workhouse (itself a useful correc-
tive to the latent historiographical view of workhouse inmates incarcerated
against their will) on an outdoor allowance of two shillings, which was, he
maintained, totally inadequate for his needs. But as he did so, Paumier
hinted at the true reason (as he saw it) behind his persecution, stating that
he had been treated this way because: "I have been a staunch & constant
friend & approver of Mr. Onion's conduct both in & out of the
Workhouse".[45] Robert Onion, a guardian of Bethnal Green union, was
instrumental in bringing Theobald Meyrick, the workhouse master, to justice for his many transgressions. As a result, he was extremely unpopular
among his fellow guardians who preferred to back the master and only
reluctantly (and after many inquiries) dismissed him when the public
clamour became too loud to ignore.[46] Paumier was thus convinced that his
own treatment resulted from continued support of Onion. But, more than
that, he viewed himself as an important figure in bringing Meyrick down,
claiming: "I have often called upon & written to [Onion] respecting the
many & flagrant errors committed by the last Master".[47]

By the time of his second letter to the commissioners—sent, in part,
because his earlier request for "an Audience" had not been granted—
Paumier demonstrated a reforming zeal that rivalled and, if anything, out-
shone, that of Thomas Gould. In it, he listed twenty-four detailed

"suggestions" and observations to aid the new Master, Mr. Wakelin, in restoring good order in the workhouse. These, he wrote:

> are the fruits of nearly 3 years of actual Experience, unprejudiced Observation, and mature Reflection upon various Facts & Inferences occuring to the Writer whilst an Inmate of the Bethnal Green Workhouse, during the years 1862, 1863 & 1866.

His observations covered everything from the "want of sympathy, benevolence & kindness" of the guardians (which, he suggested, resulted in many of the deserving poor being dissuaded from applying for relief or admission in the first place) to the endemic corruption of workhouse officers and inmates, the harsh work regime, poor medical treatment, and a terrible diet. Similar to Gould and social investigators such as Rowntree, Paumier painstakingly identified much of the minutiae of workhouse life as contributing to the unhappiness of inmates, such as the poor quality and limited extent of the clothing, the small allowances of tobacco, the way that the wards were cleaned (constant dampness being deleterious to health, he wrote), and even the manner in which the beds were made in the morning.[48] Like Gould, Paumier's list of complaints and remedies reads more like an organised manifesto than the grumbles and grievances which we might have expected from workhouse inmates, and testifies to both sustained agency and a wider awareness of the temperature of contemporary public debate on the New Poor Law and its workhouses. Like Rowntree, Gould and most critics of the deterrent workhouse, Paumier wanted to reform and not replace the system.

By January 1867, Paumier was once again an inmate of the workhouse and was writing to the commissioners to complain of the situation he found there. This time, he accused the new workhouse master of starving not only the paupers, but his subordinate officers as well, whilst at the same time feeding his own family on "Turkey, Fowells &c&c". Intriguingly, Paumier declined to put his own name to this letter, merely signing it "An Inmate".[49] Whatever the reasons for his anonymity in this instance, by April he was again writing openly to the commissioners, and by August he had taken on the cause of another elderly inmate, Thomas Rosamond, who at that time was dangerously ill in the sick ward, having been forced to work outside in torrential rain. Paumier accused Baddeley, the Superintendent of Labour, of cruelty and harsh treatment against elderly residents, and he was later called to give evidence at an inquiry that was held following Rosamond's death from pneumonia. Baddeley subsequently resigned his position, an outcome that testifies to the potential for agency of an individual pauper and, as with Gould, must also have filtered through the workhouse as an example of what could be achieved by engaging with the authorities.[50]

Paumier's final letter to the commissioners, dated August 1869, was written after he had been outside the workhouse for two years, and the fact that it was written at all suggests one of the avenues through which agency might run between indoor and outdoor paupers and how workhouse conditions could become the focus of sustained public attention in local communities.[51] In it, he wrote again in great detail of the problems and issues of the workhouse. Paumier's list ran to almost 2000 words and concentrated mostly on the dietary and work regimes for elderly and infirm inmates. He was also keen to set the record straight on the practice of egregious punishment, echoing Gould more than a decade earlier: "Your Inspectors occasionally visit the Workhouse & ask the Inmates if they have any Complaints to make—But they rarely meet with any reply, because the Poor Sufferers are absolutely afraid to tell their grievances, lest they should be punished for doing so", and he went on to "earnestly entreat" the commissioners, "on behalf of the Poor Aged Sufferers, that you will kindly interfere on their account, & have them relived from some, if not from all of these grievances".[52] While many pauper writers threatened their respondents with public exposure—something we return to below—Paumier's is an important case because by the time of this 1869 letter, he was no longer an inmate himself, and in this sense, he *was* the public. This is also true of our remaining two writers.

Henry Jones, Pwllheli Workhouse

Henry Jones first wrote to the Poor Law Board in April 1868. By that time, he had already been a resident in Pwllheli workhouse for sixteen months having, by his own account, lost everything in a shipwreck following 40 years as a seaman. He stated at the beginning of his correspondence that he was effectively disabled owing to "a fall I had on Board of a ship and broke both of my feet [at] the heel Bones".[53] Just as we saw with Gould and Paumier, Jones' first task was to establish his "respectability" (and therefore, he believed, his credibility), assuring the Board that although he had been unable to work for the two years following his shipwreck he did not ask for any assistance from "the union"; but, "as old age is comming on me I feel the effects of that fall on me is getting worst [and] I am not able to Go to Sea".[54] Jones complained that when he was first admitted to the house the doctor refused to allow him anything more in his diet than the ordinary able-bodied paupers, despite the fact that he was "in a weak state previous to comming here" and was suffering from "weakness in my feet and limbs and general debility of the whole system". After three and a half months in the house "I got so weak and low that I could scarce walk". Still, the doctor refused to adjust his diet and told Jones that he was not entitled to anything by order of the guardians. He went on to complain of the poor quality, as well as the scarcity, of the food, even alleging that "in the summertime especially [...] insects and vermin crawls about our breakfast and supper is full of black beetles and earwigs enough to turn the stomach of a strong man".[55] Overall, the list of complaints in this first letter (which ran to nine sides and 3700 words) was long and, as we shall see, extended to those that affected many other paupers as well; but his overriding concerns were to do with cleanliness and the presence of "vermin" in the workhouse.

In particular, Jones complained—on behalf of himself and several other named paupers—of a lack of adequate clothing, and of the frequency with which it was laundered. He wrote that "we could seldom get our drawers and stocking changed and some of the men said that they had wore their drawers for 3½ months ... [I] myself had to wear my own flannel drawers for 7 or 8 weeks before I could get a change". This was a common complaint in many of the letters sent by paupers to the Poor Law Commissioners, and it speaks eloquently of the importance of dignity and decency to the indoor poor.[56] But according to Jones, the situation was particularly extreme at Pwllheli where "we were all in a most awful wretched state of filth and vermin that we could not rest at our work [...] for it took the most of our time to kill vermin".[57] This was a complaint that went straight to the heart of the proper treatment of indoor paupers, as the official directives relating to the exchange of pauper clothing for workhouse dress and a strict regimen of cleanliness and laundry were explicitly designed to ensure that the "vermin" (or body lice) they brought with them were not transferred to the workhouse population at large.[58] Jones then went on to suggest that the attendance on the sick and elderly poor was inadequate, just as Gould and Paumier and the social investigator Joseph Rowntree had, and that he himself had been ordered to attend sick paupers (one of whom died in his care) despite being "disabled" and patently unqualified for the role. Like the other writers in this study, Jones rehearsed these complaints several times adding more and more detailed evidence with each letter to reinforce his account. He even transcribed statements apparently taken down from other paupers to corroborate his evidence, each of which bore the mark of the putative witness. Such methods mirror exactly those of middling social investigators of this and later periods. Finally, as a result of his advocacy on behalf of other paupers, he claimed that he had been told by "one of the matrons" that "I was only a pauper here and no pauper had a right to interfere for another", following which he was abused not only by the master of the workhouse, but by the master's young daughter.[59] This, though, was just the beginning of Jones' persecution.

In his second letter, sent two months after the first, Jones claimed that, as a result of having complained to the Poor Law Board, he had been thrown out of the workhouse "on a small pittance of 1/6 [one shilling and sixpence] pr week which is not nearly enough to keep life in a man". This, of course, directly echoes Paumier's treatment at Poplar. He also alleged that the doctor had been told to deny that he was in any way disabled by his injured feet, and that the doctor was a man who "in general laughs and jeers at the poor men", even telling another elderly pauper that "it was time for him to die now as he had lived long enough".[60] Nonetheless, despite the fact that he was no longer resident in the workhouse (temporarily, as it turned out) Jones again continued to transcribe and forward yet more "statements" marked by named paupers, which reinforced the raft of accusations he had made in his earlier letter about the poor state of the food, the overall cleanliness in the workhouse, the treatment of sick paupers and, most prominently of all, the filthy and vermin-ridden state of the clothing they were allocated. One such statement even claimed that an elderly pauper had a weeping abscess, but was still forced to wash his own trousers and underclothes as no one could be found to do it for him.

It is once again clear in these letters that Jones not only wrote on behalf of many named paupers besides himself but that his complaints extended to the treatment of the workhouse poor in general (in particular the sick and elderly), and that taken together they offered—and were meant to offer—a stinging critique of the entire system of indoor relief at Pwllheli and its oversight by the guardians. Unusually, Jones self-consciously employed the language of natural justice and the rights of the citizen to emphasise his case, even turning the proud boast of the freeborn Englishman back on the commissioners.[61] "As England expects every man for to do his duty", he wrote:

and her subjects to have freedom and justice done to them without any favour to the rich more than the poor […] let my case be duly investigated and decided by a jury partly of Englishmen that I may have justice […] and not squeeze and hunger me because I wrote to you to London for justice[.] Mercy to be done to me and my countrymen which has shared and suffered with me in the said most wretched place of purgatory that is a disgrace to a civilised nation.[62]

Jones' campaign for justice was clearly informed by the long-held antipathy of the Welsh towards the distant rule of the London Commissioners.[63] But in every other respect, it followed almost to the letter those of Gould and Paumier before him, and of a wider contemporaneous critique of the deterrent workhouse. Like other paupers, Jones got his wish for an investigation into the situation at Pwllheli, and even though it was not conducted in front of a jury of Englishmen, it was at least presided over by an inspector from the Poor Law Board, Andrew Doyle, and was reported in the local press. However, it was not a formal inquiry, and (in common with our first two writers) it did not lead to the outcome Jones had hoped for, as he made clear in his next letter. "I beg to state to you", he wrote:

that I have read in the *Carnarvon and Denbigh Herald* dated 13th of June 1868 a false statement that Mr Watkins Governor of the Pwllheli workhouse made in defence of himself concerning the complaints made by me and others against him and the matron and also the medical man of the said union workhouse.[64]

Jones went on to demand that "if something will not be done soon of reformation through her Majesty's Officials concerning the said complaints they must be forwarded to Her most gracious majesty herself".[65]

Clearly, Queen Victoria was unlikely to personally endorse his campaign, but Jones' letter is significant for two reasons. The first is that he showed himself to be a reader of the press, suggestive of the growing reach of public opinion; the second is that while Jones did not see the potential for overthrowing the New Poor Law, he had a clear sense that the very pinnacle of the state would realise the need for its reform. In practice, Jones, in tandem with other advocates for the Pwllheli workhouse poor, did succeed in forcing another local inquiry by the Board of Guardians, again presided over by the Poor Law Board's inspector Andrew Doyle. Once more, however, the many charges sworn to in his letters by named paupers were briefly discussed, and summarily dismissed. Many of those who put their names to the complaints were called as witnesses, but even these could not sway the inspector, and the Chairman of the Board of Guardians concluded that "no enquiry into the charges was necessary, and it was very satisfactory now to find that there was no cause for the complaints". The meeting ended with a formal resolution "to the effect that the Guardians were satisfied with the conduct of the master and matron".[66] Jones was far from shy in letting the Poor Law Board know that these were "sham or mock inquir[ies] held at Pwllheli Union work house", and that "it is useless to me to seek or ask mercy or justice done to me and others". He had appealed directly to the national authorities in London to bring local officials to justice, but the system had failed him. He looked to the newspapers to find some vindication, but he was again thwarted by the duplicity (as he saw it) of local officers. His bitter conclusion was that "if I and others dare to have presumption to say that we are entitled to any mercy or justice in this world there is but very little shown to us here at Pwllheli".[67] Like Gould and Paumier (and, in a different context, Joseph Rowntree) he had tried to work within the system and found it wanting. Unlike them, he did not (or was not in a position to) go on to appeal to the court of public opinion, though he was aware of its (positive and negative) power. Our final pauper letter-writer did so, however; and, indeed, he went one stage further when the official channels proved inadequate.

JOHN RUTHERFORD, POPLAR WORKHOUSE

John Rutherford spent only four months in Poplar workhouse, between July and November 1885 at the height of the crusade against outdoor relief. As a result of his experiences, he wrote five letters of complaint to the Local Government Board, all of which were sent in a brief flurry of activity *after* he had left the house between 4 December and 22 December 1885. As with our other writers, in his first letter Rutherford sent a meticulously detailed list of shortcomings and failings as he saw them. This itemised list corresponds closely to Paumier's inventory of suggestions for the reform of the Bethnal Green union, hinting at least that the two men had picked up some of their suggestions from reform conversations in the periodical press. Rutherford's complaint began with the inflammatory suggestion that "no material improvement … imperatively required, is ever made in the Poplar Union Workhouse, except as the result of a Coroner's Inquest on some of the unfortunate inmates". He went on to give a "typical" example (much as did social investigators such as Seebohm Rowntree), outlining the case of an elderly pauper who had died without the comfort of his family's presence because his daughter was refused admission to attend him in his last days.[68] Rutherford then proceeded, in familiar fashion, to bemoan the state of the food given to elderly paupers (which he claimed was rancid and even rotten on occasion), the corruption and peculation of workhouse officials and trusted inmates, and, significantly, the collusion of the Board of Guardians with the general mismanagement of the workhouse. He (like Gould and Jones) accused both the Board and workhouse officers of persecuting those who complained, and of a "vindictive" refusal to investigate such complaints, no matter how serious.[69]

Although his list of grievances is very familiar, there are a number of things in Rutherford's correspondence that mark him out, even amongst our serial correspondents. For one thing, he was motivated to complain in the first place in part because of the actions of another inmate who, he claimed, had fomented the male paupers in the workhouse to "a state of hardly covert insurrection". That inmate was Frank Burge, who Rutherford described as "an ex solicitor's clerk, with whom your Honourable Board is not unacquainted".[70] Rutherford declared that Burge "did his best, first by persuasion & then by gross threats, to make me follow his lead", but that he (Rutherford) refused, placing himself "as a matter of conscience— on the side of order & good management", echoing Gould and Paumier's claims to be a positive influence in the workhouse. He went on to write that "by my own unaided […] exertions I did much to break this fellow's influence with the inmates", and that "Among other things I wrote a letter at a very critical period, which greatly strengthened the hands of the Guardians against this fellow Burge".[71] Rutherford's letter evidences the complex matrix of low-level enmities which peppered workhouse life, but it also provides some sense of the bubbling grievances that could shape the attitudes of workhouse inmates to each other and to staff, some of which might erupt episodically into unrest. In this particular case, the problem for Rutherford was that his letter was published by the guardians in the local press to weaken Burge's case against them. Despite the fact that it was published anonymously, Burge soon learned the identity of the writer and Rutherford was assaulted by Burge "and six or seven of his accomplices, in the young Men's Hall of the workhouse". He claimed that, having fought them off, Burge then turned the tables by laying a complaint against him, which the Master appears to have accepted at face value.[72]

So convoluted is Rutherford's narrative of personal and collective grievances that, at times, it is difficult to pinpoint precisely who was the real target of his complaints. Clearly, he blamed Burge—"a most cunning, mischievous & dangerous fellow"—for his role in creating disorder and division among the inmates.[73] But he also accused the workhouse officers, and particularly the master, of day-to-day deficiencies of management, and further accused the Board of Guardians of complacency and collusion. He later accused the master of fathering a child with a married female pauper, claiming that the guardians had covered up the affair by bribing the woman's husband with extra comforts. Yet, it is also clear that Rutherford was firmly on the side of the Guardians in his battle of wills with Burge: it was to them that he sent his first letter of complaint, and he also wrote that, had Burge been taken to a Police court as he suggested, "the Guardians would have been delivered for ever from the villanous pettifogger & his groundless actions for law".[74]

Rutherford muddied the waters still further in his second letter, when he noted that the master and two of his officers had been fined at Thames Police Court for assault. Instead of celebrating this as evidence of the master's bad character, he wrote that, "as a matter of duty & conscience [...] [I] give it as my firm conviction, that [...] the officers of the Workhouse were very harshly, not to say unjustly dealt with". His reason for siding with the workhouse officers in this instance was that "I know one of the complainants (Bateman) to be an ill conditioned grievance monger, whose ways are not pleasant to his fellow inmates", and who was previously "stimulated by Frank Burge" to go to the courts with "a really frivolous complaint against the Master". Bateman was, he wrote, prevented from doing so only by his (Rutherford's) intervention.[75] The restrictive and oppressive workhouse regime begins to soften somewhat when we follow these observations to their logical conclusion: pauper inmates had time for gossip and extended discussion and persuasion; some inmates—a majority is implied by Rutherford—wanted to get along with workhouse staff; and those staff must have lived in the knowledge that they could be fined and investigated whether or not the charges against them were trumped up or not. Reading the words of Rutherford, we can see that navigating the undercurrents of the workhouse was complex, but that in this endeavour the poor really did have an active and practical agency.

Rutherford's list of antagonists was long and far from straightforward, but he was aware of this himself. Following his statement against Batemen, he acknowledged that, in making it, "I am sweeping away matter that would tend to support my own charges" against the master. Nonetheless, "I disdain support of that sort", and he insisted on the veracity of the complaints, claiming (like Gould) that he was motivated only by a deep concern "for the Rate payers […] [and for] the Indoor Paupers of the Poplar Union". "I am resolved", he continued:

> in one way or another, *& in spite of all obstacles*, to put an end to the state of things obtaining yonder […] it is a state of things which enables all sorts of rascals who have any connection with the house—nay which encourages them—to prey upon the rate payers.[76]

So strong was Rutherford's determination to have the situation addressed that his requests for action strayed far beyond the usual courtesies found in appeals to the Local Government Board. In his first letter, for example, he wrote:

> I demand an investigation into the whole affair. I demand to have it ascertained why the Guardians used my letter, thus exposing me to the dangerous animosity of [Burge] […] I demand to know by what malicious or treacherous means my name, as the writer of the letter […] was communicated to him. I demand also […] [an] examination of the conduct of the Master of the workhouse in the affair.[77]

His *demands* were in themselves an extraordinary act of agency given the latent belief that the poor were powerless, and they remind us of the forthright language deployed by Jones in seeking "justice" for his fellow countrymen. Similarly, when they fell on deaf ears, Rutherford wrote that "I regret to find that the Local Government Board will not interfere with the vilest workhouse mismanagement, when compelled to do so by a great public scandal" and reiterated that "I am determined that poor men & women shall not be murdered by slow torture simply that rascally workhouse masters & guardians may fill their pockets, while those whose duty it is to check such people look smiling on".[78] Like Thomas Gould, William Paumier and Henry Jones, Rutherford's initial complaints and requests for intervention developed into a campaign in the face of what he interpreted as the complacency of officials, much as we also saw in the case of Joseph

Rowntree in Chap. 2. In the same letter, Rutherford stated that "I had meant to confine my efforts to the Poplar Union [but] I shall now extend them to the whole system", observing that "[t]his is my fourth letter to your Honourable Board, And I have given abundant time between each letter for the right sort of answer to come". He finished this final letter by stating that if his well-founded accusations were "unworthy of the notice of your Honourable Board until forced upon it by Public Opinion, I shall not trouble *you* again".[79] Rutherford was clearly aware of the power of publicity and public opinion to force changes in practice. His remarkably aggressive rhetoric here suggests that there was a strong undercurrent of such knowledge in the communities where workhouses were located, and among workhouse inmates themselves. It is to this matter that we finally turn.

WORKHOUSE "CRUSADERS" AND THE COURT OF PUBLIC OPINION

As we have seen throughout this book, our four prolific letter writers were active during a particularly turbulent period in the history of the New Poor Law. In London, the number of paupers grew dramatically between the 1850s and the 1880s, fuelled by a convergence of trade depressions, rising food prices, the influx of poor immigrants, and the impact of war.[80] Structural issues in the administration of the poor law itself also had a disproportionate effect on unions in the capital, particularly single-parish unions, such as Bethnal Green, but also other poor East End unions like Poplar.[81] In Wales, too, the period of the crusade against outdoor relief was a turbulent one, with more and more paupers being forced into inadequate and poorly-funded workhouse accommodation against the general tide of Welsh welfare policy, and very often against the wishes of paupers and ratepayers alike.[82] The net result was that unions faced huge pressures, both financially and in terms of workhouse capacity. The severity of this crisis goes some way towards explaining the increase in complaints that were received by the commissioners from inmates in union workhouses across the whole of England and Wales at this time.[83] Nonetheless, these broader currents are not sufficient in themselves to explain the extraordinary epistolary activity of our correspondents. There are, however, further clues about the context and motivation behind their activity within the letters themselves.

In his first and most detailed letter, John Rutherford sought to enlighten the commissioners with regard to serious shortcomings at the Poplar workhouse, of which he clearly believed they were ignorant. In his second, he again urged the Local Government Board to investigate matters thoroughly, believing that it was the appropriate body to do so. In a third, he observed that "the longer such charges remain uninvestigated the more favourable becomes the situation for the accused & the more unfavourable for the accuser".[84] In his final letter, Rutherford displayed a considerable impatience at the Board's inability, or unwillingness, to act. Like Gould and Paumier, Rutherford made it clear that he had "not the smallest private interest to serve by subjecting myself to the labour, worry, & animosity in which such a determination is sure to involve me".[85] At some point, though, it became clear to all of these serial letter writers that they were to be thwarted by the practical limits of the commissioners' power to demand or enforce sustained local change, just as we saw with Joseph Rowntree. Integral to their campaigns was a keen awareness of the potential for publicity and the power of the press to force recalcitrant local and national officials into action. Henry Jones looked to the papers for an exposé of the inadequacies of the guardians' administrative regime and the misconduct of the workhouse officers, but all he found there was a duplicitous statement by the master and an uncritical report of the guardians' bland resolutions, fully supported by the Poor Law Board's emissary, Andrew Doyle. The others, however, went one stage further: on realising the limits of complaint through their epistolary campaigns, they decided to circumvent the usual channels and bring their concerns to a wider audience themselves. Thomas Gould informed the commissioners that he had written an account based on his complaints, along with "many more uncontradictory facts […] which I intend to make public". Sadly, no trace of this account has been found, if it was ever published. Mungo Paumier was similarly moved to write a "full, true & particular account" of his time in Bethnal Green workhouse when he left it in 1869, which he was then "preparing for publication".[86] Again, no such account has been discovered, but he did write at least two letters to the newspapers about the state of the workhouse regime in 1871, when he was once again an inmate at Bethnal Green. The first of these was published anonymously in the *East London Observer*, and took the form of a poem entitled "'Hope Deferred;' or the Ins and Outs of it: a Workhouse Lamentation in Bethnal Green" (Fig. 3.1). Having been forced to admit to being its author, he soon wrote another letter complaining that he had been punished "for my advocacy of *truth*

WORKHOUSE POETRY.

To the Editor of the " East London Observer."

Sir,—You have so often employed your talents in defence of the poor inmates of Bethnal Green Workhouse that they hope you will once more permit them to appeal to public sympathy by inserting the annexed lines, this week, if possible.

So seriously have the health and spirits of the old folks been affected by these cruel restrictions, that many of them have *fretted themselves ill*, and been compelled to resort to the *sick wards*, where several of them have *died* ; others have been reduced to absolute despair, and some on the verge of *insanity*. Hoping that you, sir, will pity our case, and advocate our cause, we remain,

THE SUFFERING INMATES.

29th, August, 1871.

" HOPE DEFERRED ;" OR, THE INS AND
OUTS OF IT.
A Workhouse Lamentation in Bethnal Green,
25th, August, 1871.

'Tis *eight long months* since Christmas-day,
    When we were *last let out* sirs ;
So may the workhouse inmates say—
    (A tedious time, no doubt, sirs)—
Since we have been allowed to see
    Our friends, our wives, or children—
Howe'er beloved they may be—
    'Tis really bewildering.

And just so long it is since they
    Were last allowed to *visit*
Those here confined *each Wednesday*,
    Which is not right—now is it ?
Except in some few cases, where
    They think we're nearly dying,
We on the " *dangerous list* " appear,
    And oft even then denying.

And why, thus cruelly are we
    From friends and kindred par
Defrauded of *our liberty*
    'Till almost broken-hearted ?
They say it is because small-pox
    Prevails so much abroad now ;
They shut us up in this " *Poor-box*,"
    Lest we should catch it somehow.

But this is only *an excuse*,
    By doctors' combination,
Compelling those *outside* to use,
    And *pay* for Vaccination ;
For even the parish doctors who
    Vaccinate the poor have recompense ;
And for each case attended to
    They charge their regular *eighteenpence*.

A nice addition to their trade,
    By this means they obtain ;
Thus *some pounds every week* are made
    To multiply their gain.
But, tho' the epidemic has
    Decreased materially,
No better is our case. Alas !
    They will not set us free.

Altho' we have petitioned oft
    The Guardians to rescind
Their rule, their hearts are not so soft
    As to make them prove kind.
Even when we *ask* them to relent,
    Begging to be excused, they
Procrastinate, with one consent,
    Postponing till *next Tuesday*.

Each *Tuesday* comes, and then we find,
    To our surprise and sorrow,
Next Tuesday ever lags behind,
    And *never comes*, like *to-morrow*.
We know not how much longer yet
    This game may be defended ;
Or if we o'er again shall get
    Our liberty extended.

Fig. 3.1 Poem later admitted to have been written and submitted by Mungo Paumier to the *East London Observer*, 2 September 1871. (Source: © The British Library Board. All rights reserved. With thanks to The British Newspaper Archive (www.britishnewspaperarchive.co.uk)

and *justice*".[87] Paumier was not alone in using the organs of the press to publicise his complaints about workhouse administration: in fact, a cursory survey of the British Library's online newspaper collection using the basic search terms "workhouse" and "inmate" throws up seventeen letters from paupers published between 1857 and 1899 in titles published as far apart as Clerkenwell (1857), Peterborough (1876), Hull (1887) and Devon (1899).[88] This once again serves to remind us of the wider currents of published workhouse criticism which both sustained, and fed upon, the testimony of paupers themselves (*pace* Rowntree), and of the fact that paupers could exercise considerable agency in debates about their conditions, notwithstanding the orthodox view of inmates as an inert and downtrodden mass.

Uniquely, however, John Rutherford *did* complete a full-length narrative of his experiences as a workhouse inmate, which was published anonymously in January 1886 as *Indoor Paupers, by 'One of Them'*. It was recently republished with a preface by Peter Higginbotham who tells us that, in researching the book, he managed to verify that Rutherford was indeed the author and that he was paid £20 by Chatto & Windus for the manuscript.[89] In his letters to the Local Government Board, Rutherford gave further details about how he came to write his publication: "I quitted the House on the 18th of November last", he wrote, "having worked my way out by collecting materials for a book, writing that book, and finding a publisher to purchase it". He went on to state that "All this I did within four months, inside of the Workhouse & while conforming exactly to all its regulations […] I may fairly claim that such a feat has never been achieved before, & is not likely to be repeated".[90] Rutherford's claims were quite true: according to the contract with Chatto & Windus, he submitted his manuscript in early November, when he was indeed still an inmate.[91] The book is a mixture of anecdote, character study and critical reflection on the workhouse regime. It is written in the manner of an exposé, showing the deficiencies of the system through sketches based around the quotidian life of its inhabitants, though Rutherford steered clear of naming names.[92] Instead, and like others with a dislike of the deterrent workhouse, he came to a general critique of the system in his conclusion, writing that:

> the most poignant abuse of the workhouse […] is the way in which its pauper inmates are regarded by the officers. They are not esteemed as human

beings at all by these high and mighty gentry, but as creatures of a far inferior order—of less account, indeed, than the tenants of a kennel.

Rutherford's solution, briefly sketched, was that guardians and overseers should be drawn from a much wider cross-section of society, and in particular that a "fair proportion" of them should be drawn from the ranks of working men. Though not a detailed solution, it would at the time have been quite radical, and it echoed the remedy suggested by Gould almost thirty years previously, as well as the reality after 1895.[93]

But Rutherford intended his published account of workhouse life to reach the widest possible audience, and while it was written in the manner of an exposé, it was also a work of considerable literary ambition. As he told the Board, he was confident it would "reach many editions".[94] Similarly, Paumier wanted his "full, true & particular account" to reach as wide an audience as possible, for he mentioned in his letters to the Board that it would also contain "*Dramatic Sketches* [...] & numerous & appropriate *Songs* & *Poems*" (one of which, presumably, found its way into the *East London Observer*).[95] We know nothing of Gould's ambitions for his exposé other than his intention to publish it, but there is something very telling in the fact that three of our four epistolary campaigners had literary ambitions stretching beyond their voluminous correspondence with the commissioners. The fact that all four correspondents wrote so extensively to the central authorities, and that they did so with such literary brio, is a demonstration in itself of their faith in the written word as an agent for change. In the context of the mid- to late-nineteenth century, and in light of the conclusions of Chaps. 1 and 2, this is hardly surprising. Even though extended accounts of the conditions inside workhouses by paupers themselves were rare (Rutherford's may indeed have been unique) the public were becoming more and more familiar with accounts by journalists and social reformers. That our three writers tapped into this wider undercurrent of public demand is important, and demands a fuller analysis, since their experiences and aspirations get to the heart of how public opinion was formed and the consequences of changing currents of such opinion.

Following early fictional depictions of workhouse life, such as those in the novels of Charles Dickens (*Oliver Twist*) and Frances Trollope (*Jessie Phillips*), by the 1850s, there was an increasing appetite for grittier, more realistic accounts. Dickens' influence here, too, is unavoidable. As noted in Chap. 1, his publications *Household Words* and *All the Year Round* contained many portraits of workhouse life from 1850 onwards.[96] His first accounts were relatively benign, but by the time he came to publish *All the Year Round*, the tone had changed markedly. Workhouse girls were being brought up "in a manner that would only tend to increase pauperism, and [...] prostitution"; workhouse infirmaries were sterile places, more like morgues than places of care and convalescence; and the "Country Workhouse" was described as "A younger brother of the Millbank Prison [...] with a surly regret for the turnkeys and warders".[97] In March 1867, the journalistic critique of workhouses came to a head with the publication of an article in *All the Year Round* entitled, "What is Sensational?" It addressed recently reported comments in Parliament by the President of the Poor Law Board, Gathorne Hardy, suggesting that the newspapers were sensationalising the conditions and management of workhouses and that their criticisms were "wholly disproportionate to the circumstances".[98] Public opinion had, then, reached a pitch that could no longer be ignored. The article pulled no punches. It painted a vivid picture of the scene inside Parliament when Hardy took on the press, where:

> legislators [were] smugly quiet, attentive, and approving; while our orator, who is tediously fluent, well-dressed and complacent, pours forth his shameless aspersions against those who have borne disinterested testimony to the truth,

and it went on to condemn the fact that:

> Paid by the public to protect the Poor, the official representative of a costly system under which paupers starve and die can find nothing more germane to the subject of poor law reform than abuse of those who have performed the real work of his department, and but for whom, it and its salaried servants, parasites, and admirers, would have continued with folded hands and brazen front to murmur "all is well".

The writer of the article then quoted at length a devastating assessment of the overcrowding and terrible conditions to be found at Strand workhouse from the pen of its own medical officer, the workhouse reformer Joseph Rogers.[99] For a long time, it was believed that the article was the work of Joseph Parkinson, one of the magazine's regular contributors; but it has recently been suggested that, although Parkinson was commissioned to write it in the first place, Dickens himself annotated it to produce such a stinging rebuke to Hardy.[100]

We would argue that it is only in the context of the growing campaign about the state of the workhouse system which was publicly waged in the pages of mid- to late-nineteenth-century newspapers, journals and pamphlets that we can understand both the nature and the extent of the correspondence into which our paupers entered with the authorities and a desire to bring their exposés to a much wider audience when they found the commissioners unwilling to act.[101] Indeed, a year before Dickens' demolition of the "parasites" in charge of the system, in January 1866, a first-hand account of workhouse life appeared that seemed to vindicate the strategies and efforts of these workhouse campaigners. In that month, the *Pall Mall Gazette* published a three-part story which ushered in the age of modern investigative journalism.[102] James Greenwood, the brother of the *Gazette's* editor, Frederick, gained access to the Lambeth workhouse disguised as a casual pauper. Anticipating Orwell's *Down and Out in Paris and London* by almost 70 years, his account, entitled "A Night in the Workhouse", was an instant sensation and was quickly reprinted elsewhere.[103] It demonstrated that there was a place not only for social investigators who described the state of workhouses from the outside, but for detailed exposés by those who had experience of them from the inside. As Rutherford noted in the preface to his earlier book, *Sketches from Shady Places:*

> To study Shady People aright one must mix with them on an equal footing—as one of themselves in short. But it is not enough to go among them for a day or a week, or even a month.[104]

If that was true of his picaresque accounts of "Shady People" on London's streets, then who better to describe the lives of London's workhouse paupers—to the authorities in London, and to the public at large—than articulate, committed and morally cognizant citizen inmates themselves, in a conclusive act of public and private agency?

The examples of the four writers whose words have dominated this chapter suggest that the way inmates experienced and navigated workhouse life in the middle and later decades of the New Poor Law was more complex and more nuanced than much of the existing literature suggests. We have, to be sure, seen scandals, the bad behaviour of workhouse staff and guardians, punishment and the abuse of power. Yet we have also seen currents of gossip and animosity between pauper inmates, acts and processes of resistance to the exercise of power, and many of the constraints

on both the central authorities and local officials when it came to controlling the workhouse environment. We do not argue that workhouse life
was pleasant, but neither was the power of the poor law and its representa-
tives unbridled. Investigations were had and practices did change. Above
all we see a strong seam of pauper agency amongst these writers (and
many like them who wrote fewer letters), a sense that they could and
should write, on their own behalf and for others, to the central authorities.
They did not always win out, and their victories may have been episodic,
sometimes transient, and occasionally pyrrhic; but there were victories
nonetheless, and the fact of them inevitably percolated through the workhouse population and the wider community within which it was located.
This percolation was helped by the fact that none of our writers, and few
of the wider sample of letter writers that we have investigated, were lifelong workhouse residents. Indeed, three of the four writers visited or
revisited the issue of workhouse life when they were no longer part of it.
They were, in other words, conduits to the public world; they both influenced, and were influenced by, wider currents of workhouse criticism and
observation. In that world, they also clearly understood the appetite of the
public for more detailed (perhaps even sensational) tales of ordinary life.
For those who engaged with it directly, the tribunal of the public was both
a way to exercise agency on their own behalf and the behalf of others, but
also a means of self-affirmation akin to the publication of working class
autobiographies and memoirs. In an ultimate act of agency, paupers like
these, through their own accounts and by talking to those (like Joseph
Rowntree) who sought to investigate the workhouse, helped to create a
spirit of reform, which by the 1890s would help to ensure the extraction
of the deserving poor from the workhouse, the creation of benefits by
right, and the eventual demise of the New Poor Law itself.

Notes

1. For an overview of these reforms, see B. Harris, *The Origins of the British
   Welfare State: Social Welfare in England* (Basingstoke, 2004).
2. M. Crowther, *The Workhouse System: The History of an English Social
   Institution* (London, 1981), 88–112; N. Longmate, *The Workhouse: A
   Social Institution* (London, 1974), 276–291. Harris, *The Origins*,
   212–216.
3. For recent popular depictions of workhouse life, see J. Worth, *Shadows of
   the Workhouse* (London, 2005); Cathy Sharp's, two-book series, "The

Children of the Workhouse", titled *The Girl in the Ragged Shawl* (London, 2018), and *The Barefoot Child* (London, 2019); and the books emerging from Peter Higginbotham's meticulously compiled online resource: http://www.workhouses.org.uk/ (accessed 08/02/2019).

4. Crowther, *Workhouse System*, 1–2.

5. Crowther, *Workhouse System*, 84, 177; L. Hollen Lees, *The Solidarities of Strangers: The English Poor Laws and the People 1700–1948* (Cambridge, 1998), 147–151.

6. D. Englander, *Poverty and Poor Law Reform in 19th Century Britain, 1834–1914* (London, 1998), 31–32, 37–40; U. Henriques, 'How Cruel was the Victorian Poor Law?', *Historical Journal*, 9 (1968), 65–68; A. Kidd, *State, Society and the Poor in Nineteenth-Century England* (Basingstoke, 1999), 35–36.

7. J. Humphries, 'Care and Cruelty in the Workhouse: Children's Experiences of Residential Poor Relief in Eighteenth and Nineteenth Century England', in N. Goose and K. Honeyman (eds.), *Childhood and Child Labour in Industrial England: Diversity and Agency 1750–1914* (Aldershot, 2013); and J. Humphries, 'Memories of Pauperism', in S. King and A. Winter (eds.), *Migration, Settlement and Belonging in Europe, 1500s–1930s* (Oxford, 2013), 102–126.

8. D. Green, *Pauper Capital: London and the Poor Law, 1790–1870* (Farnham, 2010). Also Englander, *Poverty*, 40–42, and P. Jones and N. Carter, 'Writing for Redress: Redrawing the Epistolary Relationship under the New Poor Law', *Continuity and Change*, 34 (2019), 375–399.

9. Green, *Pauper Capital*, 157–188. The overlap between these observations and the concerns and frameworks of Joseph Rowntree are unmistakeable.

10. J. James, 'Sophia Heathfield of Hawnes, Bedfordshire: Punishment Victim or Victor?', *Family and Community History*, 21 (2018), 202–229. Alice Clark, 'Wild Workhouse Girls and the Liberal Imperial State in Mid-nineteenth Century Ireland', *Journal of Social History*, 37 (2005), 389–409, makes similar points in relation to girls in Irish workhouses.

11. S. King, 'Thinking and Rethinking the New Poor Law', *Local Population Studies*, 99 (2017), 5–19; P. Carter, J. James and S. A. King, 'Punishing Paupers? Control, Discipline and Mental Health in the Southwell Workhouse, 1836–1871', *Rural History*, 30 (2019), 161–180.

12. P. Higginbotham, *Voices from the Workhouse* (London, 2012).

13. Green, *Pauper Capital*. For context see P. Carter and S. King, 'Keeping Track: Modern Methods, Administration and the Victorian Poor Law, 1834–1871', *Archives*, 60 (2014), 31–52.

14. D. Englander, 'From the Abyss: Pauper Petitions and Correspondence in Victorian London', *London Journal*, 25 (2000), 71–83.

15. See also Green, *Pauper Capital*, 184–185 for an example from the City of London Workhouse.
16. S. King, '"It is impossible for our vestry to judge his case into perfection from here": Managing the Distance Dimensions of Poor Relief, 1800–40', *Rural History*, 16 (2005), 161–189. They were genuinely requests. No rights to receive relief existed, merely the right to apply.
17. See, for instance, P. Jones, '"I cannot keep my place without being deascent": Pauper Letters, Parish Clothing and Pragmatism in the South of England, 1750–1830', *Rural History*, 20 (2009), 21–39; S. King, 'Negotiating the Law of Poor Relief in England, 1800–1840', *History*, 96, (2011), 410–435; and T. Sokoll, 'Writing for Relief: Rhetoric in English Pauper Letters, 1800–1834', in A. Gestrich, S. King and L. Raphael (eds.), *Being Poor in Modern Europe: Historical Perspectives, 1800–1940* (Oxford, 2006), 91–111.
18. S. A. King, *Writing the Lives of the English Poor, 1750s–1830s* (London, 2019), 229–255, and C. Brant, '"The Tribunal of the Public": Eighteenth Century Letters and the Politics of Vindication', in C. Bland and M. Cross (eds.), *Gender and Politics in the Age of Letter Writing 1750–2000* (Aldershot, 2004), 15–28.
19. G. Finlayson, *Citizen, State and Social Welfare in Britain, 1830–1990* (Oxford, 1994), 92–93, and E. Hurren, *Protesting about Pauperism* (Woodbridge, 2007). Poplar and Bethnal Green became crusading unions.
20. S. and B. Webb, *English Poor Law History Part II: The Last Hundred Years* (London, 1963 repr.); P. Ryan, 'Politics and Relief: East London Unions in the Late-nineteenth and Early-twentieth Centuries', in M. Rose (ed.), *The Poor and the City: The English Poor Law in its Urban Context, 1834–1914* (Leicester, 1985), 133–172; L. Marks, 'Medical Care for Pauper Mothers and their Infants: Poor Law Provision and Local Demand in East London, 1870–1929', *Economic History Review*, 46 (1993), 518–542; Green, *Pauper Capital*, 201–241; and M. Brodie, *The Politics of the Poor: The East End of London 1885–1914* (Oxford, 2004).
21. Sokoll, 'Writing for Relief', 91–111, and M. Lyons, 'Ordinary writings or how the illiterate speak to historians', in M. Lyons (ed.), *Ordinary Writings, Personal Narratives: Writing Practices in 19th and early 20th Century Europe* (Bern, 2007), 13–32.
22. On respectability in London see L. Mackay, *Respectability and the London Poor, 1780–1870: The Value of Virtue* (London, 2013).
23. On demotic autobiography: J. Burnett (ed.), *Useful Toil: Autobiographies of Working People from the 1820s to the 1920s* (London, 1974); D. Vincent, *Bread, Knowledge and Freedom: A Study of Nineteenth Century Working Class Autobiography* (London, 1979); J. Burnett and D. Mayall, *The*

Autobiography of the Working Class (New York, 3 vols., 1984, 1987, 1989); and J. Humphries, *Childhood and Child Labour in the British Industrial Revolution* (Cambridge, 2010).

24. This "humble" opening address is common to many letters from the ostensibly weak to the actually powerful, especially those emanating from institutions. See M. Włodarczyk, 'Initiating Contact in Institutional Correspondence: Historical (socio) Pragmatics of Late Modern English Literacies', *Journal of Historical Pragmatics*, 18 (2017), 271–294.

25. On the importance of this observation about the aged in light of the composition of workhouse populations, see G. Boyer, '"Work for their prime, the workhouse for their age": Old age pauperism in Victorian England', *Social Science History*, 40 (2016), 3–32.

26. TNA MH 12/7683, Thomas Gould to the PLB, 23 August 1853. Original emphasis.

27. The flawed character of workhouse masters is a latent theme in the historiography. See L. Foster, 'The representation of the workhouse in nineteenth-century culture', (Unpublished PhD thesis, University of Cardiff, 2014), 89–132.

28. TNA MH 12/7683, Thomas Gould to the PLB, 23 August 1853. Studies of inmates via the census indicate that in terms of occupation and socio-economic standing, workhouse populations were often an eclectic mix of long-term paupers, the life-cycle poor and former ratepayers, business people and officers like these. The presence of the latter groups might make the contestation of the workhouse regime and rules more intelligible.

29. The text alludes to prior scandals and disputes. See Green, *Pauper Capital*, 201–228.

30. K. Price, *Medical Negligence in Victorian Britain: The Crisis of Care under the English Poor Law, c.1834–1900* (London, 2015).

31. TNA MH 12/7683, Thomas Gould to the PLB, 23 August 1853.

32. H. Martineau, *Poor Laws and Paupers Illustrated* (London, 1833); 'A workhouse probe', *All Year Round*, Nov. 1867; E. Shaw, 'The workhouse from the inside', *Contemporary Review*, Oct. 1899. Also, L. Foster, 'Dirt, dust and devilment: Uncovering filth in the workhouse and casual wards', *Victorian Network*, 6 (2015), 29–58.

33. TNA MH 12/7683, Thomas Gould to the PLB, 17 October 1853.

34. TNA MH 12/7683, Gould to the PLB, 9 November 1855.

35. On corruption in supply contracts see D. Brown, 'Supplying London's Workhouses in the Mid-Nineteenth Century', *London Journal*, 41 (2016), 36–59.

36. For context, see Price, *Medical Negligence*, 104–118.

37. TNA MH 12/7684, Gould to the PLB, 9 November 1855.

38. The level of detail here suggests that Gould was aware of his vulnerability and wished to leave nothing to chance when accusing union officials of wrongdoing.

39. TNA MH 12/7683, Gould to the PLB, 23 August 1853.

40. TNA MH 12/7684, Gould to the PLB, 9 December 1855.

41. TNA MH 12/7684, Gould to Lord Palmerston, 17 December 1855.

42. TNA MH 12/7684, Gould to Lord Palmerston, 17 December 1855.

43. Gould used this phrase twice in the letter, TNA MH 12/7684, Gould to the PLB, 9 November 1855. In signing it off, he noted: "nothing short of a moral duty has huryd me to this".

44. Green, *Pauper Capital*, 186, 199–201; J. Hepburn, *A Book of Scattered Leaves: Poetry of Poverty in Broadside Ballads of the Nineteenth-Century England* (London, 2000), 181–189.

45. TNA MH 12/6853, Mungo William Paumier to the PLB, 5 December 1866.

46. Hepburn, *Book of Scattered Leaves*, 181–189. Foster, 'The Representation', 130–168.

47. TNA MH 12/6853, Paumier to the PLB, 5 December 1866. Paumier's claims to have been central to the events surrounding the scandal at Bethnal Green workhouse in 1866 and 1867 appear to have some foundation. His place in these events, and the wider context of the Bethnal Green scandal, are the subject of ongoing work by the authors.

48. TNA MH 12/6853, Paumier to the PLB, 12 December 1866. As with Gould these complaints mirrored those emerging from the investigative initiatives of the 1860s including a *Lancet* commission on workhouse hospitals (1865), undercover reporting in the *Pall Mall Gazette* (1866), and an investigation of Bethnal Green workhouse itself by *The Times* in January 1866.

49. TNA MH 12/6854, Paumier to the PLB, 30 January 1867. Even though he did not sign this letter, the writing is very clearly and distinctively Paumier's own.

50. TNA MH 12/6854, Paumier to the PLB, 2 August 1867; TNA MH 12/6854, Paumier's witness statement on the death of Thomas Rosamond, August 1867; TNA MH 12/6854, Bethnal Green Guardians' internal report on the death of Thomas Rosamond, August 1867.

51. Indeed, in 1867 Paumier had been invited to address a public meeting in London Fields, Hackney, on the alleged cruel treatment of paupers in the Bethnal Green Workhouse. *Illustrated Police News*, 7 September 1867.

52. TNA MH 12/6854, Paumier to the PLB, 16 August 1869.

53. TNA MH 12/16063, Henry Jones to the PLB, 8 April 1868. There seems to have some delay between Jones beginning this first letter and its

receipt by the PLB, as the Board's date stamp registers it as having been arrived on 18 May 1868.

54. On the prevalence of aged men in workhouses, see Boyer, '"Work"'.
55. TNA MH 12/16063, Jones to the PLB, 8 April 1868.
56. On 'decency' and standards with regard to workhouse clothing, see P. Jones, S.A. King and K. N. Thompson, 'Clothing the New Poor Law Workhouse in the Nineteenth Century', *Rural History* (forthcoming, 2021).
57. TNA MH 12/16063, Henry Jones to the PLB, 8 April 1868.
58. Jones, King and Thompson, 'Clothing the New Poor Law Workhouse'.
59. TNA MH 12/16063, Henry Jones to the PLB, 8 April 1868.
60. TNA MH 12/16063, Henry Jones to the PLB, 5 June 1868.
61. On the wider context for links between poverty, poor relief and citizenship, see M. Levine-Clark, *Unemployment, Welfare and Masculine Citizenship: So Much Honest Poverty in Great Britain, 1870–1930* (Basingstoke, 2015).
62. Ibid.
63. M. Evans and P. Jones, '"A Stubborn, Intractable Body": Resistance to the Workhouse in Wales, 1834–1877', *Family and Community History*, 17 (2014), 109–116.
64. TNA MH 12/16063, Henry Jones to the PLB, 27 June 1868.
65. Ibid.
66. *Merionethshire Standard*, 1 August 1868.
67. TNA MH 12/16063, Henry Jones to the PLB, 13 May 1868.
68. TNA MH 12/7698, John Rutherford to the Local Government Board (LGB), 4 December 1885.
69. Ibid.
70. Ibid. Burge was also a serial correspondent to the LGB, writing more than 16,000 words of complaint over a series of letters. Burge's case really is unique, which is why he does not figure in the present discussion. Nonetheless, Burge and Rutherford's careers as workhouse inmates were inextricably linked. The result was a fascinating epistolary *ménage a trois* between the two of them and the LGB which is soon to be the subject of further published work.
71. On the wider heroic narrative into which Rutherford was clearly keying, see J. Price, *Everyday Heroism: Victorian Constructions of the Heroic Civilian* (London, 2014).
72. TNA MH 12/7698, John Rutherford to the LGB, 4 December 1885.
73. Ibid.
74. Ibid.
75. TNA MH 12/7698, John Rutherford to the LGB, 7 December 1885.
76. TNA MH 12/7698, John Rutherford to the LGB, 11 December 1885. Original emphasis. Rutherford thus constructs himself as an essentially moral man of good citizenship. For context see T. Gibson-Bryden, *The*

Moral Mapping of Victorian and Edwardian London: Charles Booth, Christian Charity, and the Poor-But-Respectable (London, 2016), and Mackay, *Respectability*.

77. TNA MH 12/7698, John Rutherford to the LGB, 11 December 1885.
78. TNA MH 12/7698, John Rutherford to the LGB, 4 December 1885. One reading of the word "public" here might be that there had already been commentary on some of the matters encompassed in this complaint in the popular press.
79. TNA MH 12/7698, John Rutherford to the LGB, 24 December 1885. Considered in the round, the similarity between these letters and the plot of a serialised novel is unmistakeable.
80. Green, *Pauper Capital*, 201–205.
81. These include systemic problems in the financing of union activities, the increasing reach of irremovability, and the low staffing base of many urban unions. See Green, *Pauper Capital*, 230–231 and Price, *Medical Negligence, passim*.
82. A. Croll, "'Reconciled gradually to the system of indoor relief'": The Poor Law in Wales during the 'Crusade Against Out-Relief', c.1870–1890', *Family and Community History*, 20 (2017), 133–135; Crowther, *Workhouse System*, 79–80; Evans and Jones, "'A Stubborn, intractable Body'", 112–115.
83. See Jones and Carter, 'Writing for Redress'.
84. TNA MH 12/7698, John Rutherford to the LGB, 11 December 1885.
85. Ibid.
86. TNA MH 12/7683, Thomas Gould to the PLB, 17 October 1853; TNA MH 12/6858, Mungo Paumier to the PLB, 16 August 1869.
87. *East London Observer*, 2 September 1871 and 7 October 1871. Use of the word advocacy here is important, speaking as it does to wider currents of social work and social investigation.
88. The British Newspaper Archive, https://www.britishnewspaperarchive.co.uk/ (accessed 19/10/2019).
89. Anon [J. Rutherford], *Indoor Paupers by 'One of Them'* (London, 1886; 2013 repr.).
90. TNA MH 12/7698, John Rutherford to the LGB, 4 December 1885.
91. Higginbotham, "Introduction" to Anon, *Indoor Paupers*, 2.
92. This mode of writing must have been influenced by the accounts of workhouse life from those who entered in disguise and then wrote about their experiences in exactly this manner.
93. Anon, *Indoor Paupers*. On the composition of Boards of Guardians after the arrival of democracy in poor law elections in 1894, see King, *Women, Welfare, passim*.
94. TNA MH 12/7698, John Rutherford to the LGB, 4 December 1885 (original emphasis). Rutherford was already the author of three further

published works by the time of his admission: *The Troubadours: Their Loves and their Lyrics* (London, 1873); *The Secret History of the Fenian Conspiracy: Its Origin, Objects and Ramifications* (London, 1877, 3 volumes); and *Sketches from Shady Places* (London, 1879), published under the pen-name "Thor Fredur". F. Boase, *Modern English Biography: Supplement (Vol. 3), L-Z* (London, 1916, repr. 1953), argues that the John Rutherford who authored the first two books was also the pseudonymous author of *Sketches from Shady Places* (Thor Fredur is an anagram of Rutherford). The literary and linguistic content in *Sketches* is so close in style and content to that found in *Indoor Paupers* that it is very unlikely they were not by the same author.

95. This language once again echoes the literary and investigative agenda on workhouses emerging from the 1860s.

96. 'A Walk in the Workhouse', *Household Words*, 25 May 1850, 204–207. See also Anon [Charles Dickens], 'The Uncommercial Traveller', *All the Year Round*, 18 Feb. 1860, 392–396; Anon, 'The Girl from the Workhouse', *All the Year Round*, 18 Oct. 1862, 132–136; Anon, 'Ill in a Workhouse', *All the Year Round*, 16 Sept. 1865, 176–179; Anon [J. C. Parkinson], 'A Country Workhouse', *All the Year Round*, 14 Dec. 1867, 16–20; Anon [J. C. Parkinson], 'A Workhouse Probe', *All the Year Round*, 30 Nov. 1867, 541–545; Anon [J. C. Parkinson], 'Another Workhouse Probe', *All the Year Round*, 7 Dec. 1867, 558–564.

97. 'The Girl from the Workhouse', 135; 'Another Workhouse Probe', 563; 'A Country Workhouse', 17.

98. Anon [J. C. Parkinson/Charles Dickens], 'What is Sensational?', *All the Year Round*, 2 Mar. 1867, 221–224.

99. Ibid. On Rogers, see Price, *Medical Negligence*, esp. part 1.

100. 'Charles Dickens revealed as author of essay defending "sensational" newspaper reporting', *Independent* newspaper, 13 Jul. 2015.

101. Something Dickens also noted by in his response to Hardy and, of course, by Rowntree.

102. S. Donovan and M. Rubery, 'Introduction', in S. Donovan and M. Rubery (eds.), *Secret Commissions: An Anthology of Victorian Investigative Journalism* (London, 2012), 17, 22–23.

103. Anon [James Greenwood], 'A Night in the Workhouse', *Pall Mall Gazette*, 12, 13 and 15 Jan. 1866. The article was subsequently reprinted elsewhere, including *The Times*, the *Birmingham Daily Post* and the *Belfast News-Letter*, as well as in pamphlet form. L. Seaber, 'Learning by Actual Experience: James Greenwood and the Birth of a Genre', in L. Seaber, *Incognito: Social Investigation in British Literature* (Cham, 2017), 17, 52.

104. Fredur [John Rutherford], *Sketches*, vi.

CHAPTER 4

Bearing Witness and Thinking Again

Abstract Our fourth chapter reflects broadly on the deep chronological roots of criticism of the deterrent workhouse, but its major focus is on the progress, nature and meaning of the workhouse reform movement developing in earnest from the 1850s. We argue that a latent sense in the popular and historiographical literature of the workhouse as a grim, crushing, monolithic and disempowering institution that could only change under the sledgehammer of scandal is unconvincing. Commentators who sustained a critique of the deterrent workhouse over more than 150 years, social investigators like Joseph Rowntree, and the paupers and potential paupers who contested their treatment and care made sure that this was so; and their efforts were played out, and were supposed to play out, in the arena of public opinion. The letters of Joseph Rowntree and serial pauper letter writers like Mungo Paumier were never meant to end up as items of archival interest, even though they are. Rather, they were meant to address, shape and sustain public opinion at a time when models of citizenship, personal responsibility for poverty, democracy and personal rights and duties were themselves changing in the face of that same public opinion.

The workhouse is undoubtedly *the* iconic institution of nineteenth-century England. Yet its place in the fabric of the New Poor Law was contested: at the ideological level in the press, pamphlet literature and political debate; at the operational level by social investigators, poverty

© The Author(s) 2020
P. Jones, S. King, *Pauper Voices, Public Opinion and Workhouse Reform in Mid-Victorian England,*
https://doi.org/10.1007/978-3-030-47839-1_4

experts and newspaper reporters and their informants; and at the client level by paupers inside and outside the workhouse who were seemingly unafraid to bring their lived concerns to a wider public by the later nineteenth century. Sometimes that public forum was alive with discussions of intense scandal. This observation—easy to trace in the digitised newspaper collections that have become more comprehensive over the last two decades—has motivated many welfare historians to view the workhouse in a largely negative light, and some to argue that totemic scandals in the early years of the New Poor Law generated such public and political outrage that policy had to be changed and (sometimes) the very administrative apparatus was disbanded and re-formed.[1] We have approached the workhouse from a different angle, suggesting that to break apart the New Poor Law workhouse from its deterrent predecessors under the Old Poor Law is to miss the significance of a long-term seam of criticism which makes the public construction of the post-1834 workhouse legible and shaped the form of that construction in important ways. Thus, while not overwhelming, from the early eighteenth century we can trace a consistent but complex thread of negative sentiment about and towards the deterrent workhouse. There were schemes to make wholesale changes to the basic canvas of the Old Poor Law well before 1834, but few gained sustained traction. In practice, most of those who criticised the Old Poor Law workhouse aimed their pens at practical issues—who should be cared for "indoors"? How was demoralisation of the impotent poor to be avoided? What should be the conditions imposed in return for relief?—rather than questioning the need for an institutional framework in the first place. Like their nineteenth-century counterparts, critics found (and sometimes manufactured) scandals in abundance, but the outcome of such scandals was invariably a set of ideas for reforming the operation of the system. In this sense, the sustained public criticism of workhouses that dominated the early years of the New Poor Law and the developing reform movement that we have traced to the 1850s and 1860s are in reality only moments in a longer and bigger story.[2] Scandals, the central lens of much excellent work on the character and role of welfare post-1834, are simply not intelligible outside of this continuum of discussion, debate and dissent.

Nonetheless, in the core chapters of this volume we have argued that the pace, depth and meaning of the public discussion surrounding workhouses *does* change from the 1850s onwards, a period which has figured remarkably lightly in the normative chronologies of the New Poor Law. The everyday conditions of short- and long-term workhouse inmates—across a spectrum from the "harmless" lunatic who spent a life in the institution to the "casuals" who might only spend a night there— attracted increasingly close scrutiny. The staff (and the Boards of Guardians who stood over them) were not invariably found wanting in this direct and often sophisticated scrutiny. Yet many were.[3] And the fact of their being found wanting, in a process epitomised here and more generally by the work of dogged social investigators like Joseph Rowntree of Leeds points to an emergent sense of what the base standards for workhouse residents should be. For Rowntree, some of those standards were clearly indicated by the rules and regulations set by the centre and frequently modified in small or tiny ways (with the assent of the centre), by localities. Yet he had other yardsticks, some backward looking and others colourfully current at the time he was gaining access to the workhouses that some guardians would rather had remained closed to him: natural justice, decency, Christian philanthropy, rights, dignity and (particularly in light of a grow- ing sense that much poverty was structural rather than the result of per- sonal failings) humanity.[4] Rowntree's simultaneous engagement with local actors and the press was a strategy also common to other investigators, as was his episodic direct action on the part of the wronged poor. Less com- mon perhaps was his dogged pursuit of the central authorities, who he accused of failing to implement, maintain and update their own rules.[5] Like many of the paupers who also wrote to the central authorities, Rowntree was convinced that a failure of inspection represented a failure of will, something that could only be rectified by the pressure of public opinion given that the poor had no really organised lobby groups.[6] In turn, it is easy to assume that this direct and recurrent pressure on policy- makers was less effective than the big scandals that have become landmarks of the early and mid-New Poor Law periods.[7] Yet, in the research for this volume and more widely, what is striking is how few abuses and infringe- ments of workhouse rules by staff and guardians magnified into full-blown "scandals" as historians have understood them, and how often (or how strategically) the central authorities intervened with local inspections and inquiries. Such local interventions, difficult to find without a thorough consideration of the central records as we suggest, are largely unheralded in the literature on the New Poor Law and yet they frequently nudged local guardians into concerted action.[8] The workhouse environment was changed by inch and degree, much less so by scandalous explosions.

A workhouse reform movement was not, of course, unified in a single line of criticism. Nor did change always garner sustained traction. As the composition of Boards of Guardians changed, staff moved between work-houses (to a much greater degree in fact than historians have ever appreciated[9]), central authority staffing was increased or diluted, and press attention shifted to other aspects or areas of the New Poor Law, the "gains" that people like Joseph Rowntree sought could be reversed. Notably (but not exclusively) in the largest urban unions, an inquiry and consequent changes to workhouse regimes might result in short-term changes before exactly the same issues reared their heads again. Indeed, some of the poor writers we encountered in Chap. 3 make exactly that point. This failure of institutional learning is not unusual, and we also see a familiar tendency for staff under the New Poor Law who were implicated in scandals to pitch up in other roles in the same sector (and sometimes the same role but in a different place). But by the 1850s and thereafter, the workhouse was firmly on the public agenda. Workhouse Visiting Societies, poverty experts, amateur social investigators (London-based, but also increasingly provincial) and everyday advocates for the poor who wrote simultaneously to Boards of Guardians, the central authorities, political figures and newspapers, sought to gain sustained attention for "progress" within the conceptual and philosophical confines of the New Poor Law. Indeed, one might argue that reaching the limits of those confines, and the realisation of just how narrow they were in the first place, are key reasons propelling England and Wales into the international convergence of thinking and speaking about the causes of poverty and appropriate welfare solutions from the 1880s onwards.[10] The point for this volume, however, is that a workhouse reform agenda *did* gain a key place in public sentiment, as might have been predicted by the presence of long-term concerns about the role and purpose of the deterrent workhouse stretching back to the 1720s.

But the public articulation of this agenda was in one sense more "democratic" by the 1850s. To suggest or assume that the very poorest elements of society were illiterate in the eighteenth and early nineteenth centuries would be to ignore a considerable body of work that points to the contrary.[11] Nonetheless, there is substantial evidence that Martyn Lyons' model of the democratisation of writing in mid-nineteenth-century Europe also applied to England and Wales, and that it was accompanied by increasingly easy ways (publication of autobiographies, letters to news-papers, petitions and letters to the central authorities, the systematic for-mulation of mechanisms of complaint for those encountering governmental and institutional processes) by which the words, opinions and sentiments of ordinary people could reach the powerful.[12] This applied to both local and state power. The extraordinary set of poor writers we encountered in Chap. 3 was clearly part of this movement. They drew upon new knowledge of poverty and workhouse abuses, public opinion in newspapers, and manifestos (latent and active) for workhouse reform, using this material to shape their writing. But it was "their" writing rather than merely a repetition or an assemblage of the views and demands of others. These men must have been a thorn in the side of the workhouse staff and Boards of Guardians who had to deal with them. It is not hard to imagine the sharp intake of breath when another letter was received or the sigh of relief when they subsequently left the workhouse. On the other hand, such men, as we have seen, were also active critics of workhouse regimes once they had left the institution and were in fact themselves members of "the public". From their words and agendas we get an insight, long forgotten but crucially important, of the interplay between public opinion, the views of the poor and their communities and the nature and fluidity of local policy. These men often suffered for their cause, as so many whistle-blowers do even today, but they also gained traction both as a result of their actions and because they were an intimate part of the matrix of people who formed the workhouse reform movement of the later nineteenth century. We make the point in Chap. 3 that such writers did not see their position or attitudes as different from the majority of workhouse inmates. More than this, while the number and depth of the letters they wrote were remarkable, many other paupers entered into epistolary contestation of the workhouse. Sometimes they wrote prodigiously and encouraged advocates to write on their behalf. All of them believed that they had a right to correspond, and many of these writers found fault with the wider system rather than just their individual treatment or the regime of the workhouse they occupied. In this, they used much the same language, conceptual framework and strategy as Joseph Rowntree and other amateur social investigators. They were complementary parts of the workhouse reform movement.

Against this backdrop, a latent sense in the popular and historiographical literature of the workhouse as a grim, crushing, monolithic and disempowering institution that could only change under the sledgehammer of scandal is less convincing. The commentators who sustained a critique of the deterrent workhouse over more than 150 years, social investigators like Joseph Rowntree, and the paupers and potential paupers who had contested their allowances and care (inside and outside institutions) in traceable ways since at least the 1750s, made sure that this was so. And their efforts were played out, and were supposed to play out, in the arena of public opinion. The letters of Joseph Rowntree and serial pauper letter writers like Mungo Paumier were never meant to end up as items of archival interest, even if one of the first tasks of the central authorities was in fact to set up a navigable and comprehensive archive of their work and the correspondence that they and others sent and received.[13] Rather, they were meant to address, shape and sustain public opinion at a time when models of citizenship, personal responsibility for poverty, democracy and personal rights and duties were themselves changing in the face of that same public opinion. In turn, the material that we have restored to the "public" realm opens up many significant new research agendas: paupers and social investigators wrote in extraordinarily emotional terms of the abuses they suspected, witnessed and sometimes manufactured, and yet we have no emotional history of the workhouse. Social investigators relied on the testimony of paupers, at least in part, and yet we know little or nothing of this relationship, beyond our account of Rowntree's interaction with Thomas Burke in Chap. 2. Indeed, were it not for our wider project on the New Poor Law from below, the activities of Joseph Rowntree would likely have remained unknown. Our pauper writers (and many others we could have cited) were not submissive. Rather they demonstrate considerable knowledge of the poor law system and the legislation that lay behind it, and a striking agency which demands further analysis.[14] Above all, we can begin to see a real sense of selfhood, and yet we have no models of the pauper self in which to ground such observations. Joseph Rowntree explicitly talked about a sense of community amongst paupers, and our pauper writers provide evidence for the existence of both supportive and antagonistic groups within workhouses; yet these are concepts that have only the most fleeting of presences in the wider historiographical literature. Moreover, while it may not be easily traceable, there is an inescapable sense that the poor—that is, current and former residents of the workhouse and those on the margins of it—were in touch with the views of the workhouse reform movement that we have identified and the press commentary that sustained it.[15] They knew, in other words, that they were not alone, and this must have influenced the way that they constructed, navigated and contested the workhouse regimes to which they were notionally subject. Yet, if there is much to do, there is also much that has been achieved here. While acknowledging scandal, abuse and casual neglect, it is time to rewrite the sentimental history of the New Poor Law workhouse.

Notes

1. For instance, S. A. Shave, '"Great inhumanity": scandal, child punishment and policy making in the early years of the New Poor Law workhouse system', *Continuity and Change*, 33 (2018), 339–363.

2. This story also encompassed reforming language, practice and agendas in other areas of "social reform", as Lawrence Goldman ably suggests: 'Social reform and the pressure of "progress" on Parliament 1660–1914', *Parliamentary History* (2018), 72–88.

3. Shave, '"Great inhumanity"', 356 suggests that post-1841 central rules were specifically *designed* to make individuals, not the system, responsible for abuse.

4. Goldman, 'Social reform', 73, argues that such yardsticks were also brought to bear in other areas of social thought and action.

5. Though as S. Richardson, 'Conversations with Parliament: Women and the politics of pressure in nineteenth-century England', *Parliamentary History*, (2018), 35–51, p. 46, notes female activists and investigators used the evidence gathering functions of select committees to put pressure on the centre.

6. On lobbying interests in the press see C. McGrath, 'British lobbying in newspaper and parliamentary discourse, 1800–1950', *Parliamentary History*, (2018), 226–249.

7. Not least, because the connections are difficult to make in a central archive running to many thousands of huge volumes of correspondence.

8. Though see Shave, '"Great inhumanity"', 350 and 354, for discussion of a similar point.

9. The revolving door for staff dismissed or severely censured has been episodically noted in the literature, but no work has yet been done on the employment and re-employment of workhouse officers across the board. See, for example, M. A. Crowther, *The Workhouse System: The History of an English Institution* (London, 1981), 120; S. A. Shave, *Pauper Policies: Poor Law Practice in England, 1780–1850* (Manchester, 2017), 226.

10. E. P. Hennock, *The Origin of the Welfare State in England and Germany, 1850–1914: Social Policies Compared* (Cambridge, 2007) and J. Harris, 'Political thought and the welfare state, 1870–1940: An intellectual framework for British social policy', *Past and Present*, 135 (1992), 116–141.

11. See most recently, S. A. King, *Writing the Lives of the English Poor, 1750s–1830s* (London, 2019).

12. M. Lyons, *The Writing Culture of Ordinary People in Europe, c.1860–1920* (Cambridge, 2013) and R. Crone, 'Educating the labouring poor in nineteenth century Suffolk', *Social History*, 43 (2018), 161–185.

13. P. Carter and S. King, 'Keeping Track: Modern Methods, Administration and the Victorian Poor Law, 1834–1871', *Archives*, 60 (2014), 31–52.

14. Though see Shave, '"Great inhumanity"', 354, for the suggestion that there was "personal and physical distance" between the poor and those who enforced policy.

15. E. P. Hennock, 'The measurement of urban poverty: From the metropolis to the nation, 1880–1920', *Economic History Review*, 40 (1987), 208–227, p. 212, argues that this was first and foremost a function of the London press, which had obtained a determined "hold … over the attention of the educated nation". In practice, as we have shown, this was a rather wider phenomenon.

Bibliography

Primary Sources

Acts, Guides and Circulars

W. G. Lumley, *The Master and Matron of the Workhouse* (2nd ed., London, 1869).

W. G. Lumley, *The Poor Removal and Union Chargeability Acts* (London, 1865).

W. G. Lumley, *The Law of Parochial Assessments Explained* (2nd ed., London, 1853).

The General Consolidated Order Issued by the Poor Law Commissioners (London, 1847).

The General Consolidated and Other Orders of the Poor Law Guardians and the Poor Law Board (6th ed., London, 1868).

The General Orders of the Poor Law Commissioners, the Poor Law Board, and the Local Government Board Relating to the Poor Law (London, 1898).

The National Archives

MH 12/6058.

MH 12/6853.

MH 12/6854.

MH 12/7683.

MH 12/7684.

MH 12/7698.

MH 12/16063.

© The Author(s) 2020
P. Jones, S. King, *Pauper Voices, Public Opinion and Workhouse
Reform in Mid-Victorian England*,
https://doi.org/10.1007/978-3-030-47839-1

NEWSPAPERS AND PERIODICALS

All Year Round.
Belfast News-Letter.
Bentley's Miscellany.
Birmingham Daily Post.
Bradford Observer.
Bury Times.
Cardiff Times.
Carlisle Journal.
Carmarthen Reporter.
Contemporary Review.
Coventry Herald.
Dundee, Perth and Cupar Advertiser.
Durham County Advertiser.
East London Observer.
Evening Mail.
Exeter and Plymouth Gazette.
Exeter Weekly Times.
Gloucester Journal.
Household Words.
Huddersfield Chronicle.
Illustrated Police News.
Journal of the Workhouse Visiting Society.
Justice of the Peace, and County, Borough, Poor Law Union, and Parish Law Recorder.
Lancaster Gazette.
Lancet.
Leeds Mercury.
Leicestershire Mercury.
Liverpool Echo.
Liverpool Mail.
Liverpool Mercury.
Lloyd's Weekly Newspaper.
London Daily News.
London Evening Standard.
Manchester Courier.
Merionethshire Standard.
Morning Advertiser.
Morning Post.
Newcastle Daily Mail.
Newcastle Guardian and Tyne Mercury.

Norfolk Chronicle.
North and South Shields Gazette.
Northampton Mercury.
Nottingham Daily Express.
Pall Mall Gazette.
Poor Man's Guardian.
Potter's Electric News.
Preston Chronicle.
Rochdale Observer.
Sheffield and Rotherham Independent.
Suffolk Chronicle.
The Express.
The Gentleman's Magazine.
The Globe.
The Independent.
The Sun.
The Tablet.
The Times.
West Kent Guardian.
Worcestershire Chronicle.
York Gazette.

Printed Primary Sources

Anon [J. Rutherford], *Indoor Paupers by 'One of Them'* (London, 1886; 2013 repr.).
J. T. Becher, *The Antipauper System; Exemplifying the Positive and Practical Good, Realised under the Frugal, Beneficent, and Lawful, Administration of the Poor laws* (2nd ed., London, 1834).
T. Bernard, *An Account of a Cottage and Garden near Tadcaster* (London, 1797).
J. Bosworth, *The Necessity of an Antipauper System, shown by an Example of the Oppression and Misery Produced by the Allowance System* (London, 1829).
C. D. Brereton, *An Inquiry into the Workhouse System and the Law of Maintenance in Agricultural Districts* (Norwich, 1826).
Damnation! Eternal Damnation to the Fiend-Begotten, "Coarser Food" New Poor Law. A Speech by Richard Oastler (London, 1837).
T. Fredur, *Sketches from Shady Places* (London, 1879).
J. Howard, *An Account of the Principal Lazarettos in Europe* (London, 1791).
H. Martineau, *Poor Laws and Paupers Illustrated* (London, 1833).
G. Rose, *Observations on the Poor laws and on the Management of the Poor in Great Britain* (London, 1805).
J. Rutherford, *The Secret History of the Fenian Conspiracy: Its Origin, Objects and Ramifications* (London, 1877, 3 volumes).

J. Rutherford, *The Troubadours: Their Loves and their Lyrics* (London, 1873).
J. Shaw (ed.), *The Loes and Wilford Poor Law Incorporation, 1765–1826* (Woodbridge, 2019).
H. Smithers, *Liverpool: Its Commerce, Statistics and Institutions* (Liverpool, 1825).
L. Twining, 'Workhouse Cruelties', *Nineteenth Century*, 20 (1886), 709–14.

Secondary Sources

B. Althammer, 'Roaming Men, Sedentary Women? The Gendering of Vagrancy Offenses in Nineteenth-Century Europe', *Journal of Social History*, 51 (2018), 736–59.
B. Althammer, 'Controlling Vagrancy: Germany, England and France, 1880–1914', in B. Althammer, L. Raphael and T. Stazic-Wendt (eds.), *Rescuing the Vulnerable: Poverty, Welfare and Social Ties in Modern Europe* (Oxford, 2016), 187–211.
I. Anstruther, *The Scandal of the Andover Workhouse: A Documentary Study of Events, 1834–1847* (London, 1973).
J. V. Beckett, 'Politics and the implementation of the New Poor Law: The Nottingham Workhouse controversy', *Midland History*, 41 (2016), 201–23.
A. Beier, '"'Takin' it to the streets": Henry Mayhew and the language of the underclass in mid-nineteenth-century London', in A. Beier and P. Ocobock (eds.), *Cast Out: Vagrancy and Homelessness in Global and Historical Perspective* (Athens, OH, 2008), 88–116.
J. Black, *The English Press, 1621–1861* (Stroud, 2001).
F. Boase, *Modern English Biography: Supplement (Vol. 3), L-Z* (London, 1916, repr. 1953).
N. Boberg Fazlić and P. Sharp, 'North and south: Long run social mobility in England and attitudes towards welfare', *Cliometrica*, 12 (2018), 251–76.
A. Borsay and B. Hunter (eds.), *Nursing and Midwifery in Britain since 1700* (Basingstoke, 2012).
J. Boulton, 'Indoors or Outdoors? Welfare Priorities and Pauper Choices in the Metropolis under the Old Poor Law, 1718–1824', in C. Briggs, P. Kitson and S. Thompson (eds.), *Population, Welfare and Economic Change in Britain 1290–1834* (Woodbridge, 2014), 143–88.
J. Boulton, 'Double Deterrence: Settlement and Practice in London's West End, 1725–1824', in S. A. King and A. Winter (eds.), *Migration, Settlement and Belonging in Europe, 1500s–1930s* (Oxford, 2013), 54–80.
G. Boyer, '"Work for their prime, the workhouse for their age": Old age pauperism in Victorian England', *Social Science History*, 40 (2016), 3–32.
J. Bradhsaw and R. Sainsbury (eds.), *Getting the Measure of Poverty: The Early Legacy of Seebohm Rowntree* (Aldershot, 2000).

L. Brake & M. Demoor (eds.), *Dictionary of Nineteenth-Century Journalism in Great Britain and Ireland* (Gent, 2009).

C. Brant, '"The tribunal of the public": Eighteenth century letters and the politics of vindication', in C. Bland and M. Cross (eds.), *Gender and Politics in the Age of Letter Writing, 1750–2000* (Aldershot, 2004), 15–28.

R. Breton, 'Portraits of the poor in early nineteenth century radical journalism', *Journal of Victorian Culture*, 21 (2016), 168–83.

M. Brodie, *The Politics of the Poor: The East End of London, 1885–1914* (Oxford, 2004).

M. Brodie, 'Artisans and dossers: The 1886 West End riots and the East End casual poor', *London Journal*, 24 (1999), 34–50.

D. Brown, 'Workers, workhouses, and the sick poor: Health and institutional health care in the long nineteenth century', *Journal of Urban History*, 43 (2017), 180–88.

D. Brown, 'Supplying London's Workhouses in the Mid-Nineteenth Century', *London Journal*, 41 (2016), 36–59.

A. Brundage, *The Making of the New Poor Law: The Politics of Inquiry, Enactment and Implementation 1832–39* (New Brunswick, NJ, 1978).

J. Burnett (ed.), *Useful Toil: Autobiographies of Working People from the 1820s to the 1920s* (London, 1974).

J. Burnett and D. Mayall, *The Autobiography of the Working Class* (New York, 3 vols., 1984, 1987, 1989).

K. Callanan Martin, *Hard and Unreal Advice: Mothers, Social Science and the Victorian Poverty Experts* (Basingstoke, 2008).

P. Carter, J. James and S. A. King, 'Punishing Paupers? Control, Discipline and Mental Health in the Southwell Workhouse, 1836–1871', *Rural History*, 30 (2019), 161–80.

P. Carter and D. Wileman, 'Managing useless work: The Southwell and Mansfield hand crank of the 1840s', in P. Carter and K. Thompson (eds.), *Pauper Prisons, Pauper Palaces: The Victorian Poor Law in the East and West Midlands 1834–1871* (Kibworth Beauchamp, 2018), 37–56.

P. Carter and S. King, 'Keeping Track: Modern Methods, Administration and the Victorian Poor Law, 1834–1871', *Archives*, 60 (2014), 31–52.

P. Carter and N. Whistance, *Living the Poor Life: A Guide to the Poor Law Union Correspondence, c.1834 to 1871* (London, 2011).

A. Clark, 'Wild Workhouse Girls and the Liberal Imperial State in Mid-nineteenth Century Ireland', *Journal of Social History*, 37 (2005), 389–409.

R. G. Cowherd, 'The Humanitarian Reform of the English Poor Laws from 1782 to 1815', *Proceedings of the American Philosophical Society*, 104 (1960), 329–32.

A. Croll, '"Reconciled Gradually to the System of Indoor Relief": The Poor law in Wales during the Crusade Against Out-Relief, c.1870–1890', *Family and Community History*, 20 (2017), 121–44.

R. Crone, 'Educating the labouring poor in nineteenth century Suffolk', *Social History*, 43 (2018), 161–85.

V. Crossman, 'Welfare and Nationality: The Poor Laws in Nineteenth-Century Ireland', in J. Stewart and S. A. King (eds.), *Welfare Peripheries: The Development of Welfare States in Nineteenth and Twentieth Century Europe* (Bern, 2007), 67–96.

M. A. Crowther, 'The Workhouse', *Proceedings of the British Academy*, 78 (1992), 183–94.

M. A. Crowther, *The Workhouse System 1834–1929: The History of an English Social Institution* (London, 1981).

L. Darwen, 'Workhouse Populations of the Preston Union, 1841–61', *Local Population Studies*, 93 (2014), 33–53.

T. Deane, 'Late Nineteenth-Century Philanthropy: the Case of Louisa Twining', in A. Digby and J. Stewart (eds.), *Gender, Health and Welfare* (London, 1996), 122–42.

S. Donovan and M. Rubery, 'Introduction', in S. Donovan and M. Rubery (eds.), *Secret Commissions: An Anthology of Victorian Investigative Journalism* (London, 2012).

F. Driver, *Power and Pauperism: The Workhouse System 1834–1884* (Cambridge, 1993).

P. Dunkley, *The Crisis of the Old Poor Law in England, 1795–1834: An Interpretive Essay* (New York, 1982).

N. Durbach, *Many Mouths: The Politics of Food in Britain from the Workhouse to the Welfare State* (Cambridge, 2020).

A. Eccles, *Vagrancy in Law and Practice under the Old Poor Law* (Abingdon, 2012).

N. Edsall, *The Anti-Poor Law Movement, 1834–44* (Manchester, 1971).

D. Englander, 'From the Abyss: Pauper Petitions and Correspondence in Victorian London', *London Journal*, 25 (2000), 71–83.

D. Englander, *Poverty and Poor Law Reform in 19th Century England: From Chadwick to Booth* (Abingdon, 1998).

M. Evans and P. Jones, '"A Stubborn and Intractable Body": Resistance to the Workhouse in Wales, 1834–1877', *Family and Community History*, 17 (2014), 101–21.

P. Fideler, *Social Welfare in Pre-Industrial England: The Old Poor Law Tradition* (Basingstoke, 2006).

G. Finlayson, *Citizen, State and Social Welfare in Britain, 1830–1990* (Oxford, 1994).

W. Forsythe, *The State of Prisons in Britain 1775–1900* (London, 8 vols., 2000).

L. Foster, 'Dirt, dust and devilment: Uncovering filth in the workhouse and casual wards', *Victorian Network*, 6 (2015), 29–58.

L. Foster, '"Probing" the Workhouse in All the Year Round', in H. Mackenzie and B. Winyard (eds.), *Charles Dickens and the Mid-Victorian Press, 1850–1870* (Kindle eBook: Buckingham, 2013).

S. Fowler, *The Workhouse* (London, 2014).

O. Frankel, *States of Inquiry: Social Investigation and Print Culture in Nineteenth-Century Britain and the United States* (Baltimore, 2006), 28–70.

O. Frankel, 'Scenes of commission: Royal commissions of inquiry and the culture of social investigation in early Victorian Britain', *The European Legacy*, 4 (1999), 20–41.

M. Freeman, 'Victorian Philanthropy and the Rowntree's: The Joseph Rowntree Charitable Trust', *Quaker Studies*, 7 (2003), 193–213.

M. Freeman, '"Journeys into poverty kingdom": complete participation and the British vagrant, 1866–1914', *History Workshop Journal*, 52 (2001), 99–121.

A. Gillie, 'The origin of the poverty line', *Economic History Review*, 49 (1996), 715–30.

T. Gibson-Bryden, *The Moral Mapping of Victorian and Edwardian London: Charles Booth, Christian Charity, and the Poor-But-Respectable* (London, 2016).

G. Ginn, *Culture, Philanthropy and the Poor in Late-Victorian Britain* (London, 2017).

L. Goldman, 'Social reform and the pressures of "progress" on Parliament, 1660–1914', *Parliamentary History* (2018), 72–88.

J. Grande, *William Cobbett, the Press and Rural England: Radicalism and the Fourth Estate, 1792–1835* (Basingstoke, 2014).

D. Green, *Pauper Capital: London and the Poor Law, 1790–1870* (Farnham, 2010).

A. Gritt and P. Park, 'The workhouse populations of Lancashire in 1881', *Local Population Studies*, 86 (2011), 37–65.

P. Gurney, *Wanting and Having: Popular Politics and Liberal Consumerism in England 1830–1870* (Manchester, 2015).

E. Hadley, *Melodramatic Tactics: Theatricalized Dissent in the English Marketplace, 1800–1885* (Stanford, 1995).

C. Hamlin, 'Nuisances and community in mid-Victorian England: The attractions of inspection', *Social History*, 38 (2013), 346–79.

A. Hansen, 'Exhibiting Vagrancy, 1851: Victorian London and the "Vagabond Savage"', *Literary London: Interdisciplinary Studies in the Representation of London*, 2 (2004).

P. Harling, *The Modern British State* (Cambridge, 2001).

B. Harris, *The Origins of the British Welfare State: Social Welfare in England and Wales, 1800–1945* (Basingstoke, 2004).

J. Harris, 'Political thought and the welfare state, 1870–1940: An intellectual framework for British social policy', *Past and Present*, 135 (1992), 116–41.

C. Helmstadter and J. Godden, *Nursing Before Nightingale, 1815–1899* (Farnham, 2011).

E. P. Hennock, *The Origin of the Welfare State in England and Germany, 1850–1914: Social Policies Compared* (Cambridge, 2007).

E. P. Hennock, 'The measurement of urban poverty: From the metropolis to the nation, 1880–1920', *Economic History Review*, 40 (1987), 208–27.

U. Henriques, 'How Cruel was the Victorian Poor Law', *The Historical Journal*, 11 (1968), 365–71.

J. Hepburn, *A Book of Scattered Leaves: Poetry of Poverty in Broadside Ballads of the Nineteenth-Century England* (London, 2000).

M. Hewitt, *The Dawn of the Cheap Press in Victorian Britain: The End of the "Taxes on Knowledge", 1849–1869* (London, 2013).

P. Higginbotham, *Voices from the Workhouse* (London, 2012).

E Higgs, *The Information State in England: The Central Collection of Information on Citizens since 1500* (Basingstoke, 2003).

C. Hilliard, 'Popular reading and social investigation in Britain, 1850s–1940s', *Historical Journal*, 57 (2014), 247–71.

T. Hitchcock, 'The Body in the Workhouse: Death, Burial and Belonging in Eighteenth-Century St. Giles in the Fields', in M. J. Braddick and J. Innes (eds.), *Suffering and Happiness in England 1550–1850: Narratives and Representations. A Collection to Honour Paul Slack* (Oxford, 2017), 153–73.

L. Hollen-Lees, *The Solidarities of Strangers: The English Poor Laws and the People 1700–1948* (Cambridge, 1998).

E. Hurren, *Dying for Victorian Medicine: English Anatomy and its Trade in the Dead Poor, c.1834–1929* (Basingstoke, 2011).

E. Hurren, *Protesting about Pauperism* (Woodbridge, 2007).

J. Humphries, *Childhood and Child Labour in the British Industrial Revolution* (Cambridge, 2010).

J. Humphries, 'Care and Cruelty in the Workhouse: Children's Experiences of Residential Poor Relief in Eighteenth and Nineteenth Century England', in N. Goose and K. Honeyman (eds.), *Childhood and Child Labour in Industrial England: Diversity and Agency 1750–1914* (Aldershot, 2013a), 115–34.

J. Humphries, 'Memories of Pauperism', in S. King and A. Winter (eds.), *Migration, Settlement and Belonging in Europe, 1500s–1930s* (Oxford, 2013b), 102–26.

J. Innes, *Inferior Politics: Social Problems and Social Policies in Eighteenth-Century Britain* (Oxford, 2009).

J. Innes, 'The "mixed economy of welfare" in early modern England: assessments of the options from Hale to Malthus (c. 1683–1803)', in M. Daunton (ed.), *Charity, Self-Interest and Welfare in the English Past* (London, 1996), 139–80.

J. Innes, S. A. King and A. Winter, 'Settlement and Belonging in Europe, 1500–1930s: Structures, Negotiations and Experiences', in S. A. King and A. Winter (eds.), *Migration, Settlement and Belonging in Europe, 1500s–1930s* (Oxford, 2013), 1–28.

J. James, 'Sophia Heathfield of Hawnes, Bedfordshire: Punishment Victim or Victor?', *Family and Community History*, 21 (2018), 202–29.

D. J. V. Jones, '"A Dead Loss to the Community": The Criminal Vagrant in Mid-Nineteenth Century Wales', *Welsh History Review*, 8 (1976), 312–44.

P. Jones, '"I cannot keep my place without being deascent": Pauper Letters, Parish Clothing and Pragmatism in the South of England, 1750–1830', *Rural History*, 20 (2009), 21–39.

P. Jones and N. Carter, 'Writing for redress: redrawing the epistolary relationship under the New Poor Law', *Continuity and Change*, 34 (2019), 375–99.

A. Kidd, *State, Society and the Poor in Nineteenth-Century England* (Basingstoke, 1999).

S. A. King, *Writing the Lives of the English Poor, 1750s–1830s* (London, 2019).

S. A. King, 'Thinking and rethinking the New Poor Law', *Local Population Studies*, 99 (2017), 104–18.

S. A. King, 'Rights, duties and practice in the transition between the Old and New Poor Laws 1820–1860s', in P. Jones and S. A. King (eds.), *Obligation, Entitlement and Dispute under the English Poor Laws, 1600–1900* (Newcastle, 2015), 263–91.

S. A. King, 'Poverty, medicine and the workhouse in the eighteenth and nineteenth centuries', in J. Reinarz and L. Schwarz (eds.), *Medicine and the Workhouse* (Rochester, 2013), 228–51.

S. King, 'Negotiating the Law of Poor Relief in England, 1800–1840', *History*, 96 (2011), 410–35.

S. King, '"It is impossible for our vestry to judge his case into perfection from here": Managing the Distance Dimensions of Poor Relief, 1800–40', *Rural History*, 16 (2005a), 161–89.

S. A. King, *Women, Welfare and Local Politics 1880–1920: "We Might be Trusted"* (Brighton, 2005b).

J. Knott, *Popular Opposition to the 1834 Poor Law* (New York, 1986).

S. Koven, *Slumming: Sexual and Social Politics in Victorian London* (Princeton, 2004).

A. J. La Vopa, 'Conceiving a Public: Ideas and Society in Eighteenth-Century Europe', *Journal of Modern History*, 64 (1992), 79–116.

A. Levene, *The Childhood of the Poor: Welfare in Eighteenth-Century London* (Basingstoke, 2012).

M. Levine-Clark, *Unemployment, Welfare and Masculine Citizenship: So Much Honest Poverty in Britain 1870–1930* (Basingstoke, 2015).

M. Lyons, *The Writing Culture of Ordinary People in Europe c.1860–1920* (Cambridge, 2013).

M. Lyons, 'Ordinary writings or how the illiterate speak to historians', in M. Lyons (ed.), *Ordinary Writings, Personal Narratives: Writing Practices in 19th and early 20th Century Europe* (Bern, 2007), 13–32.

N. Longmate, *The Workhouse: A Social History* (London, 1974).

L. MacKay, *Respectability and the London Poor, 1780–1870: The Value of Virtue* (London, 2013).

P. Mandler, 'The Making of the New Poor Law Redivivus: Reply', *Past and Present*, 127 (1990), 194–201.

P. Mandler, 'The New Poor Law Redivivus', *Past and Present*, 117 (1987), 131–57.

L. Marks, 'Medical Care for Pauper Mothers and their Infants: Poor Law Provision and Local Demand in East London, 1870–1929', *Economic History Review*, 46 (1993), 518–42.

J. D. Marshall, 'The Nottinghamshire Reformers and their Contribution to the New Poor Law', *The Economic History Review*, New Series, 13:3 (1961), 382–96.

L. McDonald, *Florence Nightingale at First Hand: Vision, Power and Legacy* (London, 2010).

L. McDonald, *Florence Nightingale: An Introduction to her Life and Family*, Vol. 1 (Waterloo, ON, 2001).

C. McGrath, 'British lobbying in newspaper and parliamentary discourse, 1800–1950', *Parliamentary History* (2018), 226–49.

M. McKinnon, 'English Poor Law Policy and the Crusade Against Outrelief', *Journal of Economic History*, 47 (1987), 603–25.

E. Midwinter, *Social Administration in Lancashire, 1830–60: Poor Law, Public Health and Police* (Manchester, 1969).

E. Midwinter, 'State intervention at the local level: The new Poor Law in Lancashire', *Historical Journal*, 10 (1967), 106–12.

S. Morgan, 'John Deakin Heaton and the "elusive civic pride of the Victorian middle class"', *Urban History*, 45 (2018), 595–615.

I. Packer, 'Religion and the New Liberalism: The Rowntree family, Quakerism, and social reform', *Journal of British Studies*, 42 (2003), 236–57.

L. Penner, *Victorian Medicine and Social Reform: Florence Nightingale among the Novelists* (New York, 2010).

R. Porter, *London: A Social History* (London, 1994).

J. Price, *Everyday Heroism: Victorian Constructions of the Heroic Civilian* (London, 2014).

K. Price, *Medical Negligence in Victorian Britain: The Crisis of Care under the English Poor Law 1834–1900* (Basingstoke, 2015).

K. Price, '"Where is the Fault?": The Starvation of Edward Cooper at the Isle of Wight Workhouse in 1877', *Social history of Medicine*, 26 (2012), 21–37.

W. Proctor, 'Poor law administration in Preston Union, 1838–48', *Transactions of the Historic Society of Lancashire and Cheshire*, 117 (1965), 145–66.

A. Randall and E. Newman, 'Protest, Proletarians and Paternalists: Social Conflict in Rural Wiltshire, 1830–1850', *Rural History*, 6 (1995), 213–18.

R. Richardson and B. Hurwitz, 'Joseph Rogers and the Reform of Workhouse Medicine', *British Medical Journal*, 299 (1989), 1507–10.

S. Richardson, 'Conversations with Parliament: Women and the politics of pressure in nineteenth-century England', *Parliamentary History* (2018), 35–51.

R. Roberts, 'How Cruel was the Victorian Poor Law', *Historical Journal*, 6 (1963), 97–107.

L. Rose, *Rogues and Vagabonds: Vagrant Underworld in Britain 1815–1985* (London, 1985).

E. Royle, *Revolutionary Britannia? Reflections on the Threat of Revolution in Britain, 1789–1848* (Manchester, 2000).

P. Ryan, 'Politics and Relief: East London Unions in the Late-nineteenth and Early-twentieth Centuries', in M. Rose (ed.), *The Poor and the City: The English Poor Law in its Urban Context, 1834–1914* (Leicester, 1985), 133–72.

L. Seaber, *Incognito Social Investigation in British Literature: Certainties in Degradation* (Cham, 2017).

W. Selinger and G. Conti, 'Reappraising Walter Bagehot's Liberalism: Discussion, Public Opinion, and the Meaning of Parliamentary Government', *History of European Ideas*, 41 (2015), 264–91.

C. Sharp, *The Barefoot Child* (London, 2019).

C. Sharp, *The Girl in the Ragged Shawl* (London, 2018).

J. Shattock (ed.), *Journalism and the Periodical Press* (Cambridge, 2019).

S. A. Shave, '"Great Inhumanity": Scandal, Child Punishment and Policymaking in the Early Years of the New Poor Law Workhouse System', *Continuity and Change*, 33 (2018), 339–63.

S. A. Shave, *Pauper Policies: Poor Law Practice in England, 1780–1850* (Manchester, 2017).

S. A. Shave, '"Immediate Death or a Life of Torture Are the Consequences of the System": The Bridgwater Union Scandal and Policy Change', in J. Reinarz and L. Schwarz (eds.), *Medicine and the Workhouse* (Rochester, 2013a), 164–91.

S. A. Shave, 'The impact of Sturges Bourne's poor law reforms in rural England', *Historical Journal*, 56 (2013b), 399–429.

K. Siena, 'Contagion, Exclusion, and the Unique Medical World of the Eighteenth-Century Workhouse: London Infirmaries in their Widest Relief', in J. Reinarz and L. Schwarz (eds.), *Medicine and the Workhouse* (Rochester, 2013), 20–21.

P. Slack, *The English Poor Law, 1531–1772* (Cambridge, 1990).

P. Slack, 'Vagrants and Vagrancy in England, 1598–1664', *Economic History Review*, 27 (1974), 360–79.

K. D. M. Snell, *Parish and Belonging: Community, Identity and Welfare in England and Wales 1700–1950* (Cambridge, 2006).

T. Sokoll, 'Writing for Relief: Rhetoric in English Pauper Letters, 1800–1834', in A. Gestrich, S. King and L. Raphael (eds.), *Being Poor in Modern Europe: Historical Perspectives, 1800–1940* (Oxford, 2006), 91–111.

A. Tanner, 'The Casual Poor and the City of London Poor Law Union, 1837–1869', *Historical Journal*, 42 (1999), 183–206.

D. Taylor, 'Beyond the bounds of respectable society: The "dangerous classes" in Victorian and Edwardian England', in J. Rowbotham and K. Stevenson (eds.), *Criminal Conversations: Victorian Crimes, Social Panic and Moral Outrage* (Columbus, OH, 2005), 3–22.

J. S. Taylor, 'The unreformed workhouse, 1776–1834', in E. W. Martin (ed.), *Comparative Development in Social Welfare* (London, 1972), 57–84.

M. van Ginderachter, '"If your Majesty would only send me a little money to help buy an elephant": Letters to the Belgian Royal Family (1880–1940)', in M. Lyons (ed.), *Ordinary Writings, Personal Narratives: Writing Practices in 19th and early 20th Century Europe* (Bern, 2007), 69–84.

A. Vernon, *A Quaker Businessman: The Life of Joseph Rowntree, 1836–1925* (London, 1958).

D. Vincent, *Bread, Knowledge and Freedom: A Study of Nineteenth Century Working Class Autobiography* (London, 1979).

R. Vorspan, 'Vagrancy and the New Poor Law in Late-Victorian and Edwardian England', *English Historical Review*, 92 (1977), 59–81.

J. Wake, *Klienwort Benson: The History of Two Families in Banking* (Oxford, 1997).

S. Webb and B. Webb, *English Poor Law Policy* (London, 1913).

A. Wilcox, *The Church and the Slums: The Victorian Anglican Church and its Mission to Liverpool's Poor* (Newcastle, 2014).

K. Williams, *From Pauperism to Poverty* (Oxford, 1981).

M. Włodarczyk, 'Initiating Contact in Institutional Correspondence: Historical (socio) Pragmatics of Late Modern English Literacies', *Journal of Historical Pragmatics*, 18 (2017), 271–94.

J. Worth, *Shadows of the Workhouse* (London, 2005).

Unpublished Sources

T. Deane, 'The Professionalisation of Philanthropy: the case of Louisa Twining, 1820–1912' (Unpublished PhD thesis, University of Sussex, 2005).

L. Foster, 'The Representation of the Workhouse in Nineteenth-Century Culture' (Unpublished PhD thesis, University of Cardiff, 2014).

T. Hitchcock, 'The English Workhouse: A Study in Institutional Poor Relief in Selected Counties, 1696–1750' (Unpublished DPhil thesis, University of Oxford, 1985).

G. Hooker, 'Llandilofawr poor law union 1836–1886: "The most difficult union in Wales"' (Unpublished PhD thesis, University of Leicester, 2013).

L. Darwen, 'Implementing and administering the New Poor Law in the industrial north: A case study of Preston union in regional context, 1837–1861' (Unpublished PhD thesis, Nottingham Trent University, 2015).

WEBSITES

https://www.britishnewspaperarchive.co.uk/.

Joseph Rowntree Foundation's website. https://www.jrf.org.uk/about-us/our-heritage/lasting-vision-change.

http://www.workhouses.org.uk.

INDEX[1]

[1] Note: Page numbers followed by 'n' refer to notes.